MW01093051

The Athletic Scholarship Playbook
A Complete College Recruiting Roadmap for High School Athletes and Parents

by Jon Fugler

Recruit-Me
Colorado Springs, CO
719-270-1346
www.recruit-me.com

Table of Contents

Introduction

"With all the athletic scholarships handed out each year, how can my son or daughter get one?"

That's a question you might be asking. That's the question my wife and I asked several years ago when our twin sons were high school juniors, excelling in baseball.

So we embarked on a journey to get an answer. We entered a world we knew nothing about and learned a lot along the way. In the end, both of our sons were able to receive a fully paid education at the school of their choice, but it did not happen the way we had expected.

There's a lot to watch out for, and you could end up spending a huge amount of money needlessly. In these pages, you'll get an education in the recruiting process, and you'll avoid the pitfalls that many parents and student-athletes fall into.

You might be feeling overwhelmed, confused or even fearful as you enter this recruiting world. I can relate. I've been there.

This book is designed to be your guide for the entire recruiting process. I want to wipe out any confusion or fears you have. This is an invaluable resource that you should come back to often.

It's your **Playbook**.

I'll teach you exactly what I've taught families for over 15 years.

For example, one Recruit-Me mom used this program to help get two of her sons recruited, one for basketball and the other for soccer.

She may have felt overwhelmed at the beginning, but when she was done she said, "Your process was easy." She referred many of her friends to my website at **www.recruit-me.com**, so I guess that's further evidence that families like you can do this successfully.

The real evidence comes in the results.

Both of her sons were recruited and had successful college careers. In fact, one son was the starting goalkeeper at his school all four years. Her other son finished "with a very strong senior season."

Another parent, William, and his daughter followed the steps I'll be showing you. By his own admission, they even started the process late.

However, they went for it. They did everything I taught them about getting her on the radar of college coaches.

"Your system worked wonderful," he said, "as she had many contacts and eventually settled on a school with the high academic standards she was looking for, as well as a full athletic scholarship, at a D1 institution."

This process was so positive for another parent, Pete, that he told me, "I might have to adopt a younger kid so I can relive the experience again!"

That's one enthusiastic dad!

Parent, would you like to see your son or daughter recruited in the next 30 days – or less?

Athlete, you can experience that.

This book lays out the process clearly, but you'll have work to do. I don't believe in complex methods, and you certainly don't need one either. You just need the dedication and commitment to follow the steps that I'll teach you.

You'll save time, money and energy by following the process I will guide you through. You could hire a service or consultant, but in most cases, there is no need to pay them thousands of dollars to get recruited.

At a fraction of the cost, parents and athletes, you can do most everything these services do – if you're willing to do the work.

One of the dads I was coaching through the process said that families often think that the club or high school coach will help promote their athlete.

"Not always true," he said. "I've seen it first-hand. You (player and parents) select what's best for you. You have to do the work. Don't leave it up to the coaches."

A friend reminded me the other day that even with recruiting services, **you** end up doing most of the work anyway.

No matter where you are in the recruiting process, if you apply the clear steps in this book, you'll get results.

In 30 days or less, you can be on the radar of college

coaches.

But First...

Before we get started, I need to address a question that may be lurking in the back of your mind...

Jon, what makes you an expert?

In other words, you're asking, "Why should I follow you?"

I'm glad you've asked that. You should.

I've referred to my family's recruiting adventure and the great results we experienced. What I didn't tell you is what happened next.

I started getting requests from friends who wanted to know how we "did it." They were hoping their kids could get athletic scholarships, too.

All I could do for them is email all the documents we used and notes on how to do the process like we did. That's it.

Then a friend, Ron Johnston, came to me and offered to put my pile of documents and notes into a logical system that any family could use and follow.

What resulted was a 200-page manual that we advertised online. Of course, we needed a website, so we built one of those, too. That was way back in 2002.

Recruit-Me was born.

Families ordered what we called the Recruit-Me System

by the hundreds. And then by the thousands. We offered a manual, workbook, college coach interviews and several other tools as part of a complete system. You can see what Recruit-Me looks like today at www.recruit-me.com.

Almost immediately, families got results. Emails came in from all over the world from parents and athletes who told us their success stories. And that has continued year after year.

It's a complete joy to see families succeed. That's what keeps me going. Remember, I am a parent who went through the same journey you and other families are going through. You'll read some other families' stories in this book.

We've enhanced the Recruit-Me System over the years. We've added more resources. We've conducted webinars and teleseminars.

I've even developed an online course that families can go through at their own pace: Athletic Scholarship University www.AthleticScholarshipUniversity.com)

My most recent addition has been the Athletic Scholarship Podcast (www.AthleticScholarshipPodcast.com), a weekly podcast where I cover practical aspects of recruiting. I interview other experts, too. Some of the topics I've tackled are...

- The #1 Secret to Getting an Athletic Scholarship
- Three Ways to Ignite a Coach's Interest
- Recruiting Q and A
- How to Talk With College Coaches When You're Not Sure What to Say

- How to Rise to the Top
- Five Things You Must Do on a Campus Visit
- Five Places to Get Discovered
- The Emotions of the Recruiting Journey
- And dozens more, including interviews with college coaches and recruiting experts

I encourage you to download the Apple Podcast App or the Stitcher Podcast App for Android. That way, you can have every episode delivered to your device as soon as it comes out every Tuesday.

But, in all these years, I've never written a book. Finally, I felt that this was the time.

What you'll get is the best of what I've taught families since 2002.

So, that's my story. I hope that gives you confidence that you can follow me in this scholarship journey.

By the end of this book, you will know:

- How to contact coaches so they want to respond to you
- How to get recruiting letters and e-mails
- What to tell a coach about yourself, and how to do so
- How to respond when coaches phone the student-athlete
- How to save hours completing questionnaires from coaches
- Where online athlete registries fit in
- How to keep coaches interested throughout the recruiting process
- How and when to use videos

- How to utilize athletic camps and showcases
- How to keep your communications straight with dozens of coaches
- How to choose the best athletic and academic programs for you

Now, let's go for it!

Jon Fugler, Athletic Scholarship Coach
CEO, Recruit-Me
jon@recruit-me.com

www.recruit-me.com

Get My Free Companion Guide

"The 10-Point Recruiting Checklist"

10-Point Recruiting Checklist

Owning this Checklist is the start of your recruiting process. **Knowing** this Checklist is one thing—**acting on it is another**.

Use this Checklist to stay on course to an athletic scholarship.

--Jon Fugler, CEO, Recruit-Me

1. **Select the Right Schools to Contact**   Resource Link
   - Discuss parent's and student-athlete's desires and preferences.
   - Write them down.
   - Research schools.
   - Discuss your lists
   - Finalize list

2. **Build your Introductory Packet**
   - Cover letter
   - Player Profile/Resume

As you read this Playbook and take action, my free **10-Point Recruiting Checklist** is a document you'll want to have as a Companion Guide to this book.

Have you ever read a how-to book before, but you got lost in the details? It's normal. The **10-Point Recruiting Checklist** will help you come back to the core of the recruiting process.

Know and track every step of your scholarship journey. Eliminate confusion. Stay on course to an athletic scholarship.

Get your **Checklist** now at:

https://tinyurl.com/10checklist

Chapter One:

Don't Fall for the Myths About Athletic Scholarships

How can I find out what's really important in going after athletic scholarships?

As I went through the recruiting process with both my sons, I found out that there are a lot of myths. Parents like you and me, and kids like ours, believe certain things that are not true, and as a result they miss the chance to receive an athletic scholarship at the school of their choice.

My goal is to help you cut through the myths and focus on what is true and important.

Let's take a look at 10 of the biggest myths.

Myth#1: If my kid is good enough, the college coaches will find him or her.

Truth: A very small percentage of high school student-athletes receive scholarships because the coach "happened to find him or her." Only the top-line elite athletes—the top 1% or so nationally—receive enough national media recognition that they are automatically recruited without having to make an effort.

The other 99%+ have to take the initiative to contact the schools where they have an interest.

Most schools' recruiting budgets are limited, and coaches rely on you to contact them first. They don't have the time or budget to travel around the country to see your student-athlete compete. Videos, stats, references and the like become key tools for the coach in the recruiting and evaluating process.

"You aren't a recruit until a coach knows about you." –Pat Dolan, St. Cloud State Baseball

Parents, you might think that it's too self-promoting to make the initial contact with a coach and to "market" your son or daughter.

However, this is the norm. If you don't do it, other student-athletes will get the scholarship. They and their parents will have made the effort and received the attention.

Coaches these days expect you to do this. It is an accepted practice.

Myth #2: *If I'm talented, the coach can get me into the school despite poor grades.*

Truth: It's just the opposite. Poor grades shut off a coach's interest more quickly than almost anything else. Even before coaches evaluate your athletic ability, they can take a look at your GPA and SAT scores and make a decision about moving forward at that point.

I remember when my wife and I were in the stands watching our sons compete in a showcase. We were watching over a coach's shoulder as he went through the player profiles in the program and crossed off athlete after athlete. What we learned later is that he was making his first evaluation based on GPA and test scores even before watching any of the athletes compete!

Schools have minimum academic requirements and coaches usually cannot get around those minimums. It's true that they can submit a list of prospective students who are "borderline" to the Admissions office, but you need to be very close to qualifying.

All things being equal, a coach would rather pursue the student-athlete with comparable abilities but with higher grades and SAT's. It's a better investment of his time. And it's less risky, because he does not want to recruit athletes that may drop out in a year or two.

The NCAA has established what is called an Academic Progress Rate (APR), which rewards or penalizes programs depending on the team's academic progress. It comes down to the individual **student-athlete's** academic progress.

Read more about this on the NCAA website. Search "academic progress rate explained."

Myth #3: I can believe everything the coaches say and promise during the recruiting process.

Truth: Coaches realize that not all recruits will choose their college. Therefore, the coaches must over-recruit. They talk to more prospects than they have spots for. Some have a tendency to over-promise and overstate, too. The reality once you enroll is not always what was presented in an attempt to recruit you.

This is not always the case and I don't want to paint a bad picture of college coaches. Most are dedicated to their program and their athletes, as well as being honest with recruits.

But... be careful. Ask questions. Try to get to know the coach's character. Check into the coach by talking with people who may know him or her. Find out about his or her reputation. If you can, talk with current athletes on the team to get their take.

As one college coach recently told me himself, "Check everything a coach says."

Myth #4: I can wait until my senior year to look for athletic scholarships.

Truth: The school selection process can take a year or more, so start in your freshman or sophomore year.

One major college coach said he starts looking at an athlete in his sophomore year of high school.

So-- in the freshman and sophomore years, start gathering information about schools and programs. Make initial contact, and begin sending stats after competing at the Varsity or club level.

You should definitely start the process no later than the junior year. The coach is under certain restrictions on when he can contact you and how he does the recruiting. Go online to see the NCAA and NAIA Recruiting Rules.

They change often, so it's good to keep checking. In fact, I used to include detailed recruiting rules in my publications, but things change so fast from sport to sport.

Two documents you should search for on the NCAA website are the latest (1) Recruiting calendars and (2) Recruiting guides.

Myth #5: Most athletic scholarships are full rides.

Truth: It is just the opposite. Other than football and basketball, it is very rare for a student-athlete to be offered a full athletic scholarship at any school. Coaches have limited scholarships as regulated by the NCAA and NAIA. They try to stretch their scholarship dollars just as you try to stretch your education dollars.

It is good to know in advance which sports are "head count sports" and which are "equivalency sports." Head count sports only offer full scholarships.

Equivalency sports can, and do, divide them up and offer mostly partial scholarships.

Head count scholarship sports are Football (DI FBS only), Basketball (DI men's and women's), Tennis (DI women only), Gymnastics (DI women only) and Volleyball (DI women only).

The rest are equivalency sports. An athlete in these sports will likely be offered room and board, tuition, or books, or some combination of these. Be prepared to pay some money at any school where you are offered a scholarship. It will likely only be a partial scholarship.

Even if your athlete is in an equivalency sport, don't overlook additional financial aid that you may qualify for -- in the form of academic scholarships or grants. When you're making the tough decision as to which school to choose, consider the whole package, not just the athletic scholarship component.

Recent figures show that the average NCAA Division I scholarship awarded is $14,270 and Division 2 is $5,548. On the NAIA side, it is $6,603. (ScholarshipStats.com)

On the next page are the maximum number of scholarships available per team at the NCAA D1 level.

Sport	Men's	Women's
Baseball	11.7	---
Basketball	13	15
Beach volleyball	---	6.0
Bowling	---	5.0
Cross-country/track & field	12.6	18.0
Equestrian	---	15.0
Fencing	4.5	5.0
Field hockey	---	12.0
Football	85 (FBS) 63.0 (FCS)	---
Golf	4.5	6.0
Gymnastics	6.3	12
Ice hockey	18.0	18.0
Lacrosse	12.6	12.0
Rifle	3.6	---
Rowing	---	20.0
Rugby	---	12.0
Skiing	6.3	7.0
Soccer	9.9	14.0
Softball	---	12.0
Swimming and diving	9.9	14.0
Tennis	4.5	8
Triathlon	---	5.5
Volleyball	4.5	12
Water polo	4.5	8.0
Wrestling	9.9	---

Myth #6: *My high school coach or guidance counselor will get me a scholarship.*

Truth: Few high school coaches or counselors have either the time or the knowledge to take charge of your recruiting process. They might have a few contacts at colleges where they can promote their exceptional athletes, but you'll need more than just a few colleges looking at you if you want the best chance of receiving a scholarship. You need to be talking to a few dozen coaches.

One father told me that his son's high school coach was "hands off," which made it harder for him to get noticed. So they contacted 50 schools themselves, had genuine interest from eight and received five offers.

This illustrates the need to keep the recruiting process in your control and don't count on others to do the job for you. Help from others is icing on the cake.

Myth #7: I have to be the best player on my team to get an athletic scholarship.

Truth: Even if you're not a national superstar already being recruited, an accomplished, talented athlete has a great chance of being recruited. But it won't just happen. Most athletes who don't reach that "blue chip" status get lost in the recruiting process UNLESS they market themselves. As I've stated, coaches rarely have the budget for massive recruiting and scouting efforts. If a college coach doesn't know you exist, they can't recruit you!

In the case of our twin sons, they were among the best on their team, but by no means the best in the county or state. Yet, they were scholarship athletes. Considering the fact that we lived in a town of 40,000 people, it makes an even stronger point.

Myth #8: Schools only give scholarships for the money sports, like football and basketball.

Truth: NCAA and NAIA schools give scholarships in almost every established sport. Though not every school offers every sport, they do make scholarship money available for a wide range of sports.

For Men: Scholarship sports include Baseball, Basketball, Cross Country, Fencing, Football, Golf, Gymnastics, Ice Hockey, Lacrosse, Rifle, Skiing, Soccer, Swimming & Diving, Tennis, Track & Field, Volleyball, Water Polo and Wrestling.

For Women: Scholarship sports include Basketball, Bowling, Cross Country, Fencing, Field Hockey, Golf, Gymnastics, Ice Hockey, Lacrosse, Rifle, Rowing, Skiing, Soccer, Softball, Swimming & Diving, Tennis, Track & Field, Volleyball and Water Polo.

In addition, new sports like Archery, Badminton, Equestrian, Handball, Rugby, Squash and Synchronized Swimming are starting to emerge at the NCAA level. As they grow, you will see more athletic scholarship money for these sports as well.

Myth #9: Coaches resent being contacted by high school athletes.

Truth: On the contrary, coaches hope to hear from good athletes who are interested in their program. They have to constantly re-fill their rosters with new athletes because every year their seniors graduate. In addition, some of their athletes graduate early and others transfer.

Coaches keep busy doing their most important job — coaching -- and rarely do they have the time or budget to discover every promising athlete on their own.

As I mentioned earlier, some blue-chip athletes come to

a coach's attention through scouting services or media exposure. However, there aren't enough of them to fill a roster. Plus, there's a lot of competition to recruit them.

Coaches want to hear from good prospects. When you contact them, you're making their job easier.

Myth #10: *I've received a letter from a coach, so I'm being recruited.*

Truth: Coaches send out hundreds of letters and emails to athletes they know little about. There are likely hundreds of student-athletes receiving the exact same letter or email you did.

Why? Because the coaches want to find out who's interested, so they **can** begin a recruiting dialogue, look at stats, and evaluate the prospects.

Conclusion

Parents, let me say few words about scholarships. Your son or daughter may have an interest in schools that do not offer athletic scholarships but have a strong academic program. Also, some schools may initiate contact but do not offer scholarships. For instance, Ivy League schools do not offer athletic scholarships, and neither do Division III schools. However, many of the non-scholarship schools are some of the best academic institutions in the nation.

The good news is that schools that do not offer athletic scholarships usually offer other forms of

financial aid, such as academic scholarships and grants. If your student is really interested in a school that doesn't offer athletic scholarships, check with that school and find out what other avenues are available. It is conceivable that they may be able to offer a financial aid package where you can pay **less** for the education than you would with a partial athletic scholarship at another school.

In fact, even if your student-athlete does receive athletic scholarship offers, you should make sure you also pursue those other financial aid options.

The recruiting and school selection process is more than pursuing the goal of getting a scholarship. You ultimately want to choose a school where you can compete and where you can get the best education—for the best price.

Parents and athletes, be thinking long-term. An athletic scholarship is a means to an end. Your scholarship enables you to get an education and prepares you for your life ahead. I doubt it will include competing professionally in 10 years.

And one more thing before we get started...

You must commit time to this.

Parents, your son or daughter has his or her hands full with academics and athletics. It is important that they do their best in these two areas, because their ability to get scholarship offers depends on it.

You need to lead your son or daughter to contact schools, write letters and emails, respond to coaches' inquiries and track the communication.

It's a big job, and will get complex as more and more coaches respond.

Athlete, this can be an overwhelming process, so you will need your parents' help and guidance – and organization. When coaches start to write and call, you can easily get consumed by the attention.

Keep on task and don't get sidetracked from your primary responsibilities: school and athletics.

Much of the material in this book is written to the student-athlete. However, I mean for every word here to be written to the parent, as well. You will need to walk your son or daughter through each element. Thanks for keeping this in mind, because it is the difference between success and failure.

Ready...Set...Go!

One of the most frequent questions I get from families is, "When do we start the process?"

My advice is to use freshman year to educate yourself on recruiting, scholarships and colleges. Begin making contact with coaches in your sophomore year and be in full swing by your junior year. If you're a senior now and you're just getting started, you'll have to speed up the steps in this Playbook.

Now that you have some critical knowledge, let's get rolling!

DON'T FALL FOR THE MYTHS ABOUT ATHLETIC SCHOLARSHIPS

Key Points:

- There are many myths that confuse people about athletic scholarships, so you need to stay informed about what's true and what's not.

- Parents must commit their time to the recruiting process to help their son or daughter.

Discuss It:

- What myths did you believe about athletic scholarships?

- What's the most important thing you've learned from this chapter?

Chapter Two:

The Starting Line

"I discovered your system back when my oldest daughter was a sophomore in high school. While she was not a D1 caliber soccer player, she nevertheless wanted to play in college. The organization and knowledge we took away from your program allowed us to put her in front of the right coaches during her critical recruiting window.

"While many of her friends were trying to land spots on college teams, we had the process completed and wrapped up 30 days after she was accepted to her college.

"When my second daughter, a soccer goalkeeper, entered high school we used the system to get her recognized much earlier than her peers. Thanks again to what we learned, she landed a number of D1, D2 and D3 offers to play at great schools. She eventually picked a D2 school and she is happily pursuing her dream to play college soccer." --A Recruit-Me Dad

The recruiting process can be pictured as a big race. However, it's not a sprint. It's a marathon.

Just like any competition, you need to go into the recruiting experience with the right attitude. Otherwise, you'll quit after a few months of effort.

As an athlete (or parent of an athlete), you know what it takes to win on the field, court or wherever you compete. Hard work, intensity, goals, talent, determination, desire, consistency, focus and practice are just a few factors.

I want you to approach your scholarship pursuit in the same way you approach athletics. There are so many parallels, especially when it comes to attitude and hard work.

You've practiced the same athletic qualities that you'll be transferring to recruiting. If you have the mindset that this is much like your athletic competition, you'll be ahead of other recruits.

Use the same tools as you use on the field. I listed some of them above.

Take the Initiative

What happens when you let your opponent take control of the play or series – or game or match?

You get crushed. You're always on the defensive, reacting to his or her moves. You don't get the chance to give your best. Your talents and character remain hidden.

And you lose the battle.

However, when you take the initiative, you gain control of the competition. You have a better shot at dictating the outcome.

You'll win.

I remember when I was competing as a pitcher in high school and college. It was such a mind game. I had to focus with every pitch. I had to take control of the batter-pitcher duel. I had to serve up my best pitches consistently.

More than that, how I carried myself, what I said, the look on my face ... all these things had a big effect on the outcome of the battle, the inning and the game.

Recruiting requires you take the initiative. Don't wait for things to happen. In competition, if you wait, usually bad things happen.

Bob wrote me about the Recruit-Me process he and his daughter went through:

"Yes, you do the work but it's worth it in the end because you have total control and focus on your son or daughter. You don't leave it up to someone who is looking after several interests."

Tim had a similar experience. He was unwilling to turn the recruiting process over to what he called a "high-dollar" recruiting service. Many friends contracted with services and paid as much as $2,000, but Tim said he did better than most of the other families. His son signed at the school that was the best fit for him.

Like Bob, Tim said that it does take a lot of work. He said he told his son to concentrate on playing ball and getting good grades while Tim acted as his "agent."

In the recruiting world, if you wait, nothing happens.

Parent, understand that coaches are not just going to discover your son or daughter. Athlete, understand that you can't expect coaches to find you unless you reach out to them.

Here's the reality:

It's your job to recruit coaches and programs.

We have it all backwards when we think that all the recruiting is done by the college coaches.

With all that said, let's get to the starting line.

Identify Your Top Schools

The place to start the scholarship race is for the parent and athlete to agree on a list of prospective colleges and universities.

This is critical. In order to take control of the recruiting process, you need begin a campaign to selected schools where the athlete wants to compete.

It begins by building a list of schools that could be in your sweet spot. Remember, you're not waiting for random things to happen. You're taking charge of your scholarship pursuit by getting some schools in your sights.

Parents, this can be a fun process as you sit down with

your son or daughter and let him or her dream a little. I would bet that you already have your top 3-4 schools you'd like your kid to consider, but remember that this is *their* choice. While you should present the benefits of the schools you have in mind, your top schools are merely "schools on the list" as far as your son or daughter is concerned.

Get out of the house and do this important exercise. Go to a coffee shop and have a good discussion. Consider the following questions. Get your thoughts out in the open.

- ✓ Do I want to stay in-state?
- ✓ Do I want to go to a large or small school?
- ✓ What part of the country?
- ✓ How tough academically do I want the school to be?
- ✓ What am I interested in studying?
- ✓ What Conference do I want to compete in?
- ✓ Any favorite schools?
- ✓ What level – NCAA Division I, II, III; NAIA?
- ✓ How about the reputation and quality of the team?
- ✓ Does cost matter?

These are just some of the questions you'll want to discuss together. Parents, you'll get a good picture of what your son or daughter is thinking.

You may even find out that they haven't given it much thought. That's not unusual, so don't worry. My sons never thought for a moment that they'd be at the school where they ended up. (They both ended up at the same place).

By asking preliminary questions like this, you'll narrow

down the field of possibilities. For instance, parents, there's no sense exploring an out of state school if your child wants to stay close to home. These preferences will probably change over time, but this is a starting point.

Surf and Explore

Go online and take a look at schools and programs. Discuss them together. You can ask some of the above questions about specific schools when you are on their site. It's a way to get some conversation going and talk things through in a practical way, rather than hypothetically.

Student-athletes, this is a good way to start conversations with your parents about the schools you are considering.

You should also take road trips. This could be one of the most rewarding things you do together. It's not a recruiting trip, but just a chance to see what a college campus looks like, feels like, etc.

Once you have your list built, try to visit 3-4 campuses just for the experience. This is another way to move the discussion from theory to practical.

Take the official tour, watch teams compete or practice and just roam around. Call ahead so you can meet the coaches and spend time with them.

Other things you can do on a college visit are:

- Hang out in the student union or quad areas
- Talk to students

- Talk with a faculty member in your areas of interest
- Eat in the dining hall
- Have an official interview with the admissions office for the sake of the experience at least
- Walk through the dorms
- Visit some classrooms
- Visit the bookstore

If you do these things, you'll certainly get the feel of the school. It will make your trip worthwhile.

I'd even recommend keeping a journal of your visits so you can refer back to them months or years later.

I believe the entire recruiting process should be a family affair as much as possible. Spending a few hours together on the Internet and on the road is a way to make it a family process. It assures that you are all getting the same information. It leads to better discussion and wise decisions.

How many?

I recommend you develop a list of at least 20-25 schools by the time you leave the coffee shop, and eventually 40-50.

Parents, this is where your insight comes in. Your son or daughter's world of reference is probably small, so they'll only think of a few schools to put on the list. However, you likely have a bigger picture, so you will have more ideas of where you want them to look into.

Student-athletes, be open to your parents' suggestions. Plan to contact the schools they add to your list. You

31

never know what will happen. By contacting more schools you will have more options open months down the road when it is time to make the decision. There's no such thing as a list too long.

Details and contact info

To make your list, you'll need to find out which colleges and universities offer your sport, and at what division level. You'll also need to get the name of each college's head coach for your sport, and the ways you can contact him or her.

How do you get all the details for this list? I'll tell you about two ways, but in the end, I'll really recommend only one, because it's by far the easiest.

Online Research

The first way is brute force: use the Internet to do your research. Assemble your own list by visiting individual college websites and pulling the details you need. This is cumbersome, but with persistence you can build your list.

If you choose this way, then a few websites may help you.

First: UnivSearch an online directory of all US institutions. This is a directory of 9,500+ institutions, so it can be daunting. You can search alphabetically, by state and by program. Understand that there are specialty schools listed, besides NCAA and NAIA schools. Visit it at:

http://www.univsearch.com/

Each college's name is a hyperlink to a profile on the school, and the link to the school is within the profile.

The list doesn't refer to sports at all. You'll have to visit the college's website to get its athletic program details to see if they should be on your list.

Another site to look at is Unigo, which is not only a directory, but has ratings and reviews by its students. This can be valuable.

https://www.unigo.com/colleges/by-state

Still another directory to check out is College Degree.

http://www.collegedegree.com/allcolleges

Second: NCAA has a roster of its member schools online at:

http://www.ncaa.com/schools

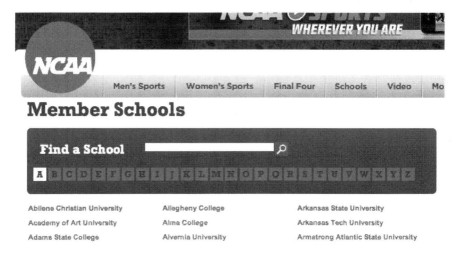

33

Third: NAIA has a roster of its member schools online at:

http://www.naia.org/ViewArticle.dbml?DB_OEM_ID=27 900&ATCLID=205322922

The Easiest Way

I want to tell you about a much more convenient tool.

College Coaches Online maintains an up-to-date directory of the over 20,000 NCAA, NAIA, and NJCAA college coaches, their sports and divisions, coach contact information, student body size, and even their cost of tuition.

This athletic database is the best, most accurate and most up-to-date registry of college and coach information available anywhere. In fact, the NCAA at one time licensed the College Coaches Online database for coach contact information, rather than attempting to maintain their own. It's that good.

Here's what I like about it. You can use the College Coaches Online Search to **identify NCAA, NAIA, or even NJCAA schools that match your criteria**. In fact, you can even narrow your search for colleges by your specific needs: location, size, tuition costs, sport, division, and your academics (grades, class rank, SAT/ACT), and within seconds you'll be given a list of all the U.S. schools that fit. The list will include the coaches' names, addresses, emails and phone numbers.

Here's an example. Let's say you're a soccer player, but you want only colleges in the **Northeast** whose **men's soccer** team competes in **NCAA Division I**. After you login, you select these criteria in the Full Search Section, then click **Find Colleges**.

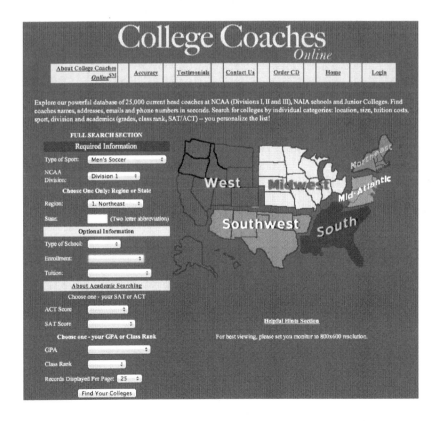

Results: Within seconds, you get a list of every college fitting your criteria. They give you each coach's name, address, email address, phone number, academic rating, and links to the school's main web page and athletic department web page. You can click on the links to read about the school and the team and decide if the school would be a good fit for you.

Sample Soccer Search Results

College Coaches
Online

About College Coaches *Online*SM	Accuracy	Testimonials	Contact Us	Order CD	Home	Login

Type of Sport: Men's Soccer		Region: 1. Northeast		Division: Division 1		New Search
|< First Group < Prev Group		Showing 1 to 25 records out of 44 found		Next Group >	Last Group >|

College Name	Coaches Name	Coaches Phone	City	State	School Type	Academic Rating
Boston College	Ed Kelly	617-552-3214	Chestnut Hill	MA	Private	1
Brown University	Pat Laughlin	401-863-2349	Providence	RI	Private	1
Colgate University	Erik Ronning	315-228-7574	Hamilton	NY	Private	1
College of the Holy Cross	Ted Priestly	508-793-2726	Worcester	MA	Private	1
Columbia University	Kevin Anderson	212-854-5436	New York	NY	Private	1
Cornell University	Jaro Zawislan	607-255-1312	Ithaca	NY	Private	1
Dartmouth College	Jeff Cook	603-646-3082	Hanover	NH	Private	1
Harvard University	Carl Junot	617-495-4549	Boston	MA	Private	1
U.S. Military Academy	Russell Payne	845-938-2463	West Point	NY	Public	1
Yale University	Brian Tompkins	203-432-1495	New Haven	CT	Private	1
Boston University	Neil Roberts	617-358-3793	Boston	MA	Private	2
Rutgers University	Dan Donigan	732-445-6223	Piscataway	NJ	Public	2
State University of New York at Binghamton	Paul Marco	607-777-4571	Binghamton	NY	Public	2
Syracuse University	Ian McIntyre	315-443-3025	Syracuse	NY	Private	2
Bryant University	Seamus Purcell	401-232-6718	Smithfield	RI	Private	3
Fairfield University	Carl Rees	203-254-4000	Fairfield	CT	Private	3
Fordham University	Jim McElderry	718-817-4269	Bronx	NY	Private	3
Manhattan College	Ashley Hammond	718-768-2017	Riverdale	NY	Private	3
Marist College	Matt Viggiano	845-575-3699	Poughkeepsie	NY	Private	3
Northeastern University	Brian Ainscough	617-373-7293	Boston	MA	Private	3
Providence College	Chaka Daley	401-865-2005	Providence	RI	Private	3
State University of New York at Buffalo	John Astudillo	716-645-3144	Buffalo	NY	Public	3
State University of New York at Stony Brook	Ryan Anatol	631-632-7203	Stony Brook	NY	Public	3
University at Albany	Trevor Gorman	518-442-3065	Albany	NY	Public	3
University of Massachusetts	Sam Koch	413-545-4341	Amherst	MA	Public	3
College Name	Coaches Name	Coaches Phone	City	State	School Type	Academic Rating
|< First Group < Prev Group		Showing 1 to 25 records out of 44 found		Next Group >	Last Group >|

Let's say you want more details about State University of New York at Buffalo, which shows that John Astudillo is the Men's Soccer Head Coach. Click on the college name hyperlink.

College Coaches Online pops up more information about the SUNY Buffalo. It plays in the Mid-American Conference. It has a student body size of 25,800. It's a public school, with In-State tuition of $7,500 and Out-Of-State tuition of $16,500, and there's more information as well.

Return to Search Results	
College Name: State University of New York at Buffalo Division of Athletics 102 Alumni Arena Buffalo, NY 14260	**Website:** http://www.buffalo.edu/ **Main Phone:** 716-645-2000
Type of Sport: Men's Soccer **Coach Name:** John Astudillo **Coach Email:** jaa@buffalo.edu **Coach Phone:** 716-645-3144	**Division:** Division 1 **Region:** 1. Northeast **Conference:** Mid-American **Nickname/Mascot:** Bulls **Athletic Website:** http://www.buffalobulls.com
Type of School: Public **Tuition Cost - In State:** 7500 **Tuition Cost - Out of State:** 16500	**Academic Rating :** 3 **School Enrollment:** 25,800
Return to Search Results	

Discount. I have a special contract with College Coaches Online that allows Recruit-Me families to **receive a $5 discount** on an annual subscription. As a disclosure, I am a College Coaches Online affiliate and receive a commission for referrals. I wholeheartedly recommend them.

Just use the code RM123 when you order at:

www.collegecoachesonline.com

THE STARTING LINE

Key Points:

- There are basic questions that student-athletes and parents should ask themselves before looking at schools, because this will help you focus on schools that are the best fit for you.

- You should contact 40-50 schools for the best long-term results, and certainly no less than 20.

- You can search out school and coach details using the Internet, or you can get a College Coaches Online subscription at www.collegecoachesonline.com. Enter the code **RM123** for a $5 discount.

Discuss It:

- As the student-athlete, which schools are at the top of your list right now?

- As the parent, which schools would you like your son or daughter to consider?

- What things are most important to you as you look for a school?

Chapter Three:

Making a Great First Impression on Coaches

"As a parent and a prospective student-athlete, you must be willing to put in the time and effort to receive your reward. A college scholarship is the prize. I have made contact with over 15 schools and received responses from each with the exception of one within one week. We look forward to the day when we can say that a scholarship has been offered and accepted. –Chris, a Recruit-Me parent.

Now that you've compiled at least a "starter list" of schools, you're ready to take the initiative and start contacting coaches.

You're going to be sending them what I call your

"Introductory Package." It will include a *Cover Letter or Email*, and a *Player Profile*. In this chapter we'll talk about the **Cover Letter**, and in chapter 5 I'll walk you through your **Player Profile** or **Resume**. Just be aware that you will need both before you're ready to contact the coaches. Don't send the Cover Letter by itself, but send it with the Player Profile.

Todd told me he and his son sent out 55 introductory packets and began receiving letters and emails within a week. His son heard from 20 coaches during that initial push, and as Todd said, "The correspondence continues to flow in." The process has opened the doors and has put his son on the radar of coaches.

"Can't I Just Contact Coaches Online?"

All college athletic programs have an online process that you can use to express your interest in their program. They have their online questionnaire just waiting for you to fill out on their websites.

See the example on the next page.

This does speed up the process, from the coach's point of view, because applicants go right into their database of prospective student-athletes.

You won't be introducing yourself using these online questionnaires. Why? Because submitting your information online takes away the personal, attention-getting nature of the process I will teach you.

How can you make a unique first impression if you are just one of dozens, or hundreds, of athletes who have submitted an impersonal online form that week?

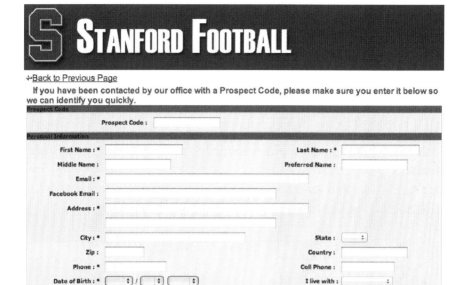

A big drawback of using an online form is that you can only give facts, figures and statistics. There's usually no way for you to describe yourself, express your enthusiasm for the school's program, or show personality. It is basically a cookie-cutter approach that makes for a much less effective first contact than sending your Introductory Package.

Therefore, I highly recommend you always send your Introductory Package to the coach before you complete their online information form. You'll make a stronger connection with the coach by doing this.

41

When the coach responds to you, he may ask you to complete his or her online form. We'll discuss that step in the chapter on Questionnaires.

The Basics of Your Cover/Intro Letter or Email

Let's go through your Cover Letter now. This is the one piece that will be able to make a personal first impression. Once you have your basic letter/email written, this will be your model for personalized letters and emails you send to colleges you are interested in.

So, a few important points about this letter.

1. **Make it *yours*.** This letter/email must come from the athlete, because that's who the coaches will want to build a relationship with. I encourage parents to help craft the letter, but make sure it's from the athlete.

2. **Make it *brief*.** The key to an effective letter can be summed up in one word: BRIEF. The goal is not to share your life story or all your great athletic achievements. That *will* come later, but a long introductory letter will turn off the coach quickly. He's only going to read the first page anyway.

Therefore...

The letter should only be **one page long**. Every word counts. This is an introduction to your student-athlete. This is an attention-grabber so the coach will be interested in looking further. The one other doc you'll be including with the letter will get into more detail.

This all makes sense, doesn't it? You'd be surprised, though, the number of parents or student-athletes who write a long letter or email that never gets read. Make a good first impression by keeping it short and interesting.

3. **Choose your words *carefully*.** You shouldn't just write whatever comes to your mind. In fact, you really need to choose your words carefully so you **communicate key elements** that will get the coach's attention. AND get his or her response.

4. **Tell the *truth*.** You need to be truthful and accurate. Don't over-inflate your accomplishments. Effectively communicate your successes that **present you in the best light**. But don't exaggerate and describe some other person. You want to be recruited for who you are.

5. **Be *interesting*.** You must communicate the kinds of things that will **get the coach's interest** and make him or her want to know more about you—enough that they write back. Don't be dull and boring by only telling facts. Let them see your heart and your passion for your sport.

The Flow of Your Intro Letter or Email

This next graphic helps you understand intuitively what should be in each section of your one-page letter or short email.

Who, what, where and when

Introduce yourself and your intentions with a one-sentence opening paragraph.

Athletic abilities

Briefly tell about three or four of your athletic accomplishments and impressive stats from your most recent season. If you have participated in or received honors in other sports, mention them, but do not include highlights.

Personal

Why do you enjoy competing in your sport? This is one, inspiring sentence from your heart.

Currently

What are you doing currently in your sport? For instance, you may be in season or playing on an off-season club team. You may be taking lessons of some kind. You may be planning to go to a summer camp in your sport. In addition, mention academics by giving your grade point average, SAT scores, or other academic achievements.

How?

How will you benefit the team you are writing to? What will you bring to the program with your abilities, skills, character and work ethic?

Parents, the following instructions are for your son or daughter as they write the letter, **with your help.**

In fact, I'll be speaking directly to your son or daughter from this point, even if you are the one leading and administrating the process.

Let's walk through the letter writing process...

A. **Who, what, where and when.** Introduce yourself and your intentions with a one-sentence opening paragraph, such as: *I am a junior in High School and I am interested in competing at Penn State in 20XX.* Here's what my son wrote in his opening paragraph:

   I have an interest in playing baseball for Ohio State next year.

B. **Athletic abilities.** Briefly tell about three or four of your athletic accomplishments and impressive stats from your most recent season. If you have participated in or received honors in other sports, mention them, but do not include highlights. He's what my son wrote in this paragraph:

   Because of my athletic abilities, I have been used as an all-around player. This summer, I played catcher and first base in addition to pitching. We played a 93-game schedule and traveled throughout several Western States. I finished 4-3 and had a batting average of .322.

C. **Personal.** Why do you enjoy competing in your sport? This is one, inspiring sentence from your heart. My son's line was not all that inspiring, but I'll let you see it anyway. He wrote:

I love baseball and because of the weather here, I can compete and condition year-round.

D. **Currently.** What are you doing currently in your sport? For instance, you may be in season or playing on an off-season club team. You may be taking lessons of some kind. You may be planning to go to a summer camp in your sport. In addition, mention academics by giving your grade point average, SAT scores, or other academic achievements. Here is what my son wrote:

Right now, I am playing on a high school travel team that competes against Junior Colleges and Scout teams in Southern and Central California. I realize that academics are a high priority, and I have kept on top of my grades, maintaining a 4.0+ GPA.

E. **How?** How will you benefit the team you are writing to? What will you bring to the program with your abilities, skills, character and work ethic? Here's what my son said:

I would bring to the Ohio State program strong abilities as a pitcher and position player, a quality work ethic and a willingness to spend time to improve. It is my dream to lead my college team to a championship.

That's it! That's all you'll be saying in your Cover Letter or email!

Email Tips

Sending your intro packet by email is customary. Your cover letter becomes the body of your email, or you can include it as an attachment.

Beware that your email can go to a coach's junk folder without you knowing it. That's the disadvantage of using email exclusively.

You can make a strong impression by regular mail, so don't count that out. Few athletes are sending things through regular mail. It's a great way to get a coach's attention!

Do the opposite of what everyone else is doing and you'll make an impression.

If a coach responds that he/she would prefer future communications by email, by all means switch to email for that coach from that point on.

Note: If you do decide to send your introductory letter by email, but do not hear back from the coach within 3-4 weeks, I recommend you send the intro packet by regular mail. Sometimes it takes that extra effort to get a coach's attention.

Positive first impression

This simple, one-page letter or short email will make a positive first impression on the coach. You'd be surprised how many people to do not send intro letters, but only a resume. I believe that the short cover letter or email gets a coach's attention by telling the student-athlete's story. It also shows that you have something on the ball.

Since many student-athletes do not send a cover letter,

and others send one as long as a mid-term report, yours will stand out. And, for athletes that use a recruiting service to contact schools for them, most of the time the service does not send a letter at all.

Remember, this must be short. That's not optional. If it is more than a one-page document, keep cutting until it is one page.

By starting with a document rather than an email, you can more easily determine that it's brief enough. Then copy and paste it into your email. Or, as I suggested, send the letter as an attachment.

I think you'll be pleased when you're done, because you'll have a hard-hitting letter with a lot of substance and no fluff.

Student-athlete, turn to your parents or an adult mentor to help you with this. You're not in it alone. You can feel overwhelmed if you're doing all the work.

Once you finish your letter, **have a couple of people read it and suggest some edits.** This is not intended to be a long process, but it's good to get a second opinion before you send it out. Remember that "first impression" priority?

When sending your introductory packet by email, then the body of your email is your cover letter. You MUST start your email with "Dear Coach Smith..." Personalize every email.

If you are sending your letter by mail, **personalize the letter and the envelope to the coach by name.** Every school has a website, so you can easily get the coach's name. The College Coaches Online database has all the coach contact information, too. If you have good handwriting, handwrite the envelope. That shows your personal interest to a coach, rather than feeling like a mass-mail campaign.

There Are Recruiting Rules

Did you know that NCAA rules allow you only five paid recruiting trips, and that you are not allowed to spend more than 48 hours on the campus?

Did you know that the NAIA allows you to work out with the team during your recruiting trip?

Be aware of the rules governing the recruiting process. You should be familiar with them.

I've included summaries of **NCAA Recruiting and Eligibility Rules** and **NAIA Recruiting and Eligibility Rules** in this book. They're written in plain English, and are both resources that will help you understand the rules. **See Appendices D and E.**

I also encourage you to visit the NCAA website at www.ncaa.org and the NAIA website at www.naia.org for the latest information.

As I mentioned earlier in the book, I've created an online course called **Athletic Scholarship University**. If you are finding at this point that you need me to lead you through the recruiting process in 3-D, then I'd encourage you to check out my online course at:

www.AthleticScholarshipUniversity.com

49

MAKING A GOOD FIRST IMPRESSION ON COACHES

Key Points:

- I absolutely highly recommend sending a personal, email or letter to the coach, even if you've completed and online form.

- Your intro letter/email should be brief, one page and just a few paragraphs.

- Write a sample or "model" letter that you can personalize for each school and coach.

- Have a couple friends or family members read your sample letter and made suggestions.

- If a coach does not respond in three weeks to your mailed letter, call him.

Discuss It:

- When will you have your sample letter completed?

- What will you set as your deadline to send your letter/email to your list of coaches?

- Parent, how can you help your son or daughter in this step in the process?

Chapter Four:

What About Online Registries?

The Internet is full of online registries where you can park your Player Profile or Resume, often for free. It seems like a great way to get exposure to college coaches. In fact, the more registries you are on, the more exposure. Or so it seems.

Let's take a look at the advantages and disadvantages of these registries, and how you can best use them for your benefit.

Advantage of Online Registries

1. **Place**. You have a place online to send coaches. An online registry can work to your advantage if **you** send coaches there. You don't have to work hard to set up a website and embed video, because it is

already done by the registry's template. In your communication with coaches, you can link to your online registry page, pictures and videos. You can also write the URL address if sending a hard copy of your letter and profile.

2. **Video hosting**. It gives you a place to host your highlight video besides YouTube.

3. **Views**. You may get some views by coaches. There are coaches who do surf online registries, but this is not the norm. The great schools have much more sophisticated recruiting programs. Programs that have a hard time attracting athletes do look on registries - mostly smaller schools. You may want to compete at a smaller school. If that's the case, a registry may be a good option for you.

Disadvantages of Online Registries

1. **Few coaches**. Most coaches don't look for recruits on online registries. Coaches want to recruit athletes who are interested in their school. A coach doesn't know who is or isn't interested by viewing a profile. Most coaches consider it a waste of time.

2. **Passive**. Online registries do a poor job of attracting coaches. They are passive sites. Even sites that put out emails to coaches to get them to their sites still can't do the job that you do when you personally contact coaches and show genuine interest.

3. **Cost**. You often have to pay a fee to receive premium services from online registries. The free offer usually only includes basic services. For example, if you

want to park your highlight video there, you may have to pay for it. Might not be worth it, since you can do that for free on YouTube.

4. **Results**. Even the paid services rarely get good results. When it comes down to it, with the online registries you are counting on coaches to find you. It goes against the most important recruiting truth: *You must take the initiative.* Coaches rarely "just find" quality recruits. If you want to be considered, you have to step forward. You can't just put your profile on a website or registry and think your job is done. You must keep following the Recruit-Me steps of action to maximize your outcome.

5. **Competition**. Once the coaches get to your page, your profile is alongside hundreds, or thousands, of other athletes wanting to get recruited to play your sport, and you may get lost in the crowd. Getting lost in the virtual world is just like getting lost in the real world.

Remember: *You must take the initiative.* Only the top tier athletes get noticed without putting out the effort. But you are likely in the other 99+%. You can get lost in the crowd, so you must put forth effort to be noticed and recruited.

If you rely on registries alone, you will violate the important principle of taking the initiative. As you've learned from Recruit-Me, you can't just wait for coaches to find you and watch you perform.

The same holds true for online registries. Coaches won't just find you there, no matter what the registries promise to get you to sign up. I hear over and over from athletes who tell me that they signed up for an online registry and it didn't work. They didn't get recruited through the registry.

How to Maximize Online Registries

There *is* a role in your recruiting plan for online registries. They're useful tools that you should utilize. But you need to work them into **your** plan, not let them **become** your plan.

I recommend that, if you park your profile on an online registry, by all means point coaches there. It is the same as if you have your own website: a convenient place for coaches to look at your profile and/or video highlights.

When you contact a coach with your Introductory Package and point him or her to your online profile and video, it shows that you're interested in their school. It is a key element that could put you on their radar. The online registry is just a plus.

One Last Word

I am a big fan of personalizing your recruiting efforts. This is the same when it comes to using online registries.

The best thing you can do is build and send your own introductory packet, which includes your intro letter/email and your Player Profile/Resume. You'll get far greater results than just putting your Profile on a website or registry and hope coaches show up.

Taylor Mathis, a former scholarship athlete himself, believes the same thing.

That's why he built **Student-Athlete Websites**.

I was so impressed with Taylor's personal touch and professional product, that I now send my Recruit-Me families to his site.

You can find out more about Student-Athlete Websites on the tools page on my Recruit-Me site:

http://recruit-me.com/tools/

I guarantee you'll get personal service and a place you'll be proud to send coaches to. What makes Taylor's service unique is that you have your own website. You're not part of a mass of student-athletes on a traditional registry.

Taylor agrees with me 100% that a website itself will not get you recruited. You still have to market yourself and send coaches to your site.

WHAT ABOUT ONLINE REGISTRIES?

Key Points:

- An online registry can be a useful tool to use in your recruiting strategy.

- An online posting is not a substitute for the more proactive Recruit-Me method, but is a good support.

- An online registry can provide a nice destination to send coaches to look at your highlight video and player profile.

Discuss It:

- Do we want to use an online registry?

- Should we pay for a premium account?

Chapter Five:

Building Your One-Page Profile or Resume

You've written your letter/email and you will use it as a model for the letter/email you send to all schools – personalized to each school, of course. Your next task is to create the one-sheet "profile" which tells the coach about your abilities and achievements.

This is really a resume. It may be the first one you've ever written, but it is probably the most important piece you will send a coach. The profile will either attract the coach or cause him to set it aside.

Parents, this is another place where you need to provide guidance and direct involvement.

Elements of Your One-Page Profile/Resume

The profile is broken up into 10 sections. You can create this profile by using Word or another document program. Then you should save it as a PDF document. Each section can be a separate text box. Let's take a look at what to include in each section.

Section 1: Name

Section 2: A short **headline** that jumps off the page, communicating something unique and impressive about you. An example would be:
87 MPH fastball and 3.6 GPA. That will get the coach's attention and cause him to read further.

Section 3: Your sport; your position

Section 4: You and your family. Include the basics about yourself. Information will include:

- Address
- Phone
- E-mail address (and website if you have your information parked there)
- Year of birth
- Year of graduation
- Number of people in family
- Number of children in college when you enter
- GPA
- ACT score (if you have it)
- SAT scores (if you have them)

Section 5: School and coaches. Include the following:

- High School
- Coach

- School office phone
- Secondary coach (summer or club team)
- His or her phone number

Section 6: Physical: Height, weight, speed, strength (if data available), dominant hand (if applicable for your sport), other sports you compete in.

Section 7: A **narrative summary** of your general strengths, as well as team and league information. Also, mention other sports that you compete in.

Section 8: A narrative of **specific stats and achievements**. This is where you brag about yourself, telling the coach about everything you do well and backing it up with the stats.

Section 9: Your potential. What will you expect to achieve in the coming year? This is a good spot for a quote from a coach. It is much easier for your coach to applaud you and project your future success than you can. It is also a stronger comment when your coach is validating your potential.

Section 10: Photo. Do not use a photo of you in uniform or in competition. A photo of you in street clothes is best.

Tommy Gray	87 MPH Fastball and 3.6 GPA
Sport: Baseball **Position: Pitcher**	

Personal	
1255 W. Electric Ave. Riverside, CA 93515	
(909) 555-1212	
tgray@internet.com	
Born: 2001 Graduation: June 2019	
Number of family members: 5 Number of children in college: 2	
GPA: 3.6 SAT: 1220 ACT: 27	

School and coaches		Physical	
High School:	Riverside HS	Height: 6'1" Weight: 185 lbs	
Coach:	Aaron Williams	Speed: 6.8/60 Vertical:	
School phone:	(909) 441-1234	Bench: 240 Squat:	
Summer coach:	Jim O'Toole	Dominant hand: Left	
Phone number:	(909) 543-2344	Other sports: Basketball	

Tommy has started varsity since freshman year, increasing in wins each year (4, 6, 7). His best pitch is his fastball, but has developed an excellent change-up in the past year. Tommy competes in a tough league in the State's second highest level. Tommy has also batted over .340 in the past three seasons, earning him a spot at first base when he is not pitching. He also plays basketball.

Tommy's ERA last season was 2.21, 7-1 record, 89 K's, 11 BB, resulting in second-team selection All County. His 87 MPH fastball resulted in a strikeout average of 1.6 per inning. Excellent position player, too, at first base and outfield. He also achieved All County in his sophomore year. Was named all-league for American Legion the past two years, winning 10 games each summer. Led his team to American Legion Regionals last year.

Tommy is expected to lead the league this year in wins and strikeouts. He is also expected to make the all-academic team for third year in a row. High School coach Aaron Williams says, "Tommy is reliable, and has been my pitching choice when we needed to win the big game. He gets the strikeout when we need it, and his control is a huge asset." Wants to major in business.

The sample Profile is just a suggestion. You can change the layout of the document to whatever suits you, but remember...

*...**one page!***

Send Your Cover Letter and Profile Together as Your Introductory Package

"We sent out letters and player profiles to 28 schools two weeks ago. We have since received questionnaires from five schools, have had video requested from three of the schools and have had email contact with the coach of one of the schools.

"Four of the questionnaires came from schools from the top 10 on my son's list. The two video requests came from the #1 and #3 on the list and the email came from #3 on the list. I would say, so far so good." -Doug, a proud parent

Once you complete your *One-Sheet Profile*, you are ready to mail or email it to the schools, together with your *Cover Letter.* These make up what I call your *Introductory Package.* These are the only two documents you want to send right now. They tell the coach all he or she will need to know in order to decide how to proceed with you.

I wouldn't reject the idea of sending this by mail, even if you email it, too. Why? Because coaches receiving a mailed package are less likely to ignore it and they certainly can't click "delete". And, as I stated earlier, you eliminate the risk of an email going to the coach's junk folder.

As a reminder, when you email your Introductory Package, make the letter the personalized body of your email. Include the Player Profile as an attached file.

Once the coach responds, you can continue the conversation by email. They are most likely to respond to you that way anyway. But now you're on their radar.

61

How will the coach respond?

If you've sent your Introductory Package that gets a coach's interest, then he or she will usually respond within a couple of weeks. You will most likely receive instructions to go to the team website to complete an online questionnaire. Sometimes, the coach may ask for a video—or just call! We will discuss the questionnaire process in the next chapter.

If you do not get a response from a coach within three weeks, then there are a couple steps you should take. If you have sent your introductory letter and player profile by email, then send the letter and profile again by regular mail.

If you have sent your letter by mail, I recommend you call. Ask for a Player Questionnaire to complete or a link to one online.

Do NOT assume that the coach isn't interested just because he or she hasn't contacted you yet. Coaches are VERY BUSY, but they want to talk with good prospects.

Help them out by taking the initiative.

BUILDING YOUR ONE-PAGE PROFILE OR RESUME

Key Points:

- Your one-sheet Player Profile tells the coaches about your abilities and achievements.

- There are several formats you can use, but be sure to stick with the key information explained in this chapter

- At this point, the Player Profile and your Cover Letter are the only things you send to a coach right now.

Discuss It:

- Who should we contact for quotes about my abilities and achievements?

- What information do I **not** have that I still need to pull together to complete the Player Profile?

Chapter Six:

When and How to Use Video

At this point, I need to address a critical part of the recruiting process. Video is one of the most strategic tools you will use in your recruiting campaign. However, the majority of families introduce video too soon. Let me explain.

Most coaches will not get a chance to see you compete in person. Therefore, your video is indeed very important. But let me warn you, *do not* send a video or video link unless the coach asks for one. Coaches receive dozens of links each day or week, and most will not watch the videos until they have a sincere interest in you.

Unless they've started a file on you as a recruit, many coaches won't take the time to deal with an unsolicited video. However, since most athletes park their videos online, it is becoming easier for coaches to take a look at them more quickly than the days when they had to deal with DVDs.

That said, when a coach **asks** you for a video, then you better have one ready – either hosted online on YouTube or a hosting site.

Note: If you've gotten your recruiting drive started very late, such as in the last half of your senior year, it may pay for you to send your video link along with your Letter and Profile.

The first two elements of the video should be about **10 minutes** and look like this:

1. **Begin with a one-minute greeting,** introducing yourself, where you are from, maybe a few words about your family, a few words about what you do in your sport, and also say something unique that will cause the coach to remember you. Then give a brief overview of what is coming up on the video. It is good to write an outline or a script, and practice it several times.

   (Note: With my sons, we had to do 3-4 takes before we were happy with what we recorded).

2. **Include some highlights in competition.** Some sparkling moments. The coach will be looking at your mechanics and style. If you are a position player in baseball or softball, include several shots of your hitting, fielding, throwing, running. If you're a pitcher, include 5-6 pitches from various angles. If you're a tennis player, some serves and other shots. If you're a football player, some isolated blocks, tackles or runs.

The third element may be as long as **20-30 minutes**:

3. **Finally, for most sports, include several minutes of continuous footage.** That way, you can be seen in action in the context of competition.

Two days ago, I met a man who produces videos for all sorts of businesses and clients. He told me he had to get up the next morning and shoot a soccer game.

Then he was going to approach the parents and see how many would like to have him produce their kid's highlight video.

I'm sure he will produce a fine video. However, it can be costly, and you may need updates along the way. That will add to the expense.

If you want to hire a professional videographer and producer, that's fine. But it is not necessary. The bells and whistles are not what impress coaches. They are evaluating talent.

Producing Your Own Video

With today's digital cameras (and even phones!) along with easy video editing software on both Mac and PC, you may be able to produce the video yourself.

It does **not** need to be a professional production. Just be sure the video quality itself is clear, but fancy editing and music is a waste of time. Coaches are looking at the athlete's skills, not the skills of your video producer. It's important to keep that in mind.

Posting Your Video

You can upload your video to YouTube for free, and send the link to coaches who ask. If you're concerned with privacy, then mark the video as Unlisted. That way, only people with the link can access it.

You can also use one of the online registries, and put your video on it, although some services charge you a fee. Another option is to build your own website and embed the video there.

You can also use Student-Athlete Websites, which is a company I trust and recommend. You can find out more about them at www.recruit-me.com/tools.

WHEN AND HOW TO USE VIDEO

Key Points:

- Generally, don't send a video link unless the coach asks for one.

- A highly produced video is not important. The most important thing is that the video clearly shows your ability so the coach can make an evaluation.

Discuss It:

- Do we have video footage to make a video? If not, when can we shoot some?

- Who will put the video together and post it?

Chapter Seven:

Build Your Questionnaire

What happens when a coach receives your letter and profile? If they are interested, they will likely request that you go to their website to fill out an online questionnaire or information form.

The coach may also request a video, send you information on a camp, or send you a packet of information on the school. Any communication you receive from a coach (except a rejection) is good news. It means there is some interest and the lines of communication are open.

The questionnaire is where you tell coaches everything about yourself, and they'll certainly know whether they want to continue the recruiting process with you. Before I get into more detail, here's a quick thing to note:

NCAA Contact Rules

Coaches are restricted on when they can first contact you, and how often they can contact you, as a prospective student-athlete, so that may not happen for a while.

For the latest NCAA rules on communications with student-athletes, go to the NCAA website. I wish I could link to the specific content on contact restrictions, but the NCAA website changes frequently. You'll need to look it up on their main website at:

www.NCAA.org

Build Your Own Questionnaire

Every questionnaire you receive or see online will be slightly different. You will go crazy if you have to fill out a different one for dozens of schools.

Instead of filling out this many custom questionnaires, a better way is to create your own completed *one-page* questionnaire. You can use it to respond to any coach. It will have all the information that any coach will ask for. When they request you to complete the online questionnaire, simply email your completed one to the coach as a PDF document. You've just saved 30-60 minutes for *each* school. That's a huge time savings when you're interacting with dozens of schools.

Once coaches show interest in you, then you can go to the website to complete the questionnaire. But it is not wise to do that at the beginning of your recruiting campaign. It takes too long.

The questionnaire I will help you build will be detailed and include the information the coaches are looking for.

What Your Questionnaire Should Include

How will you know what information to include? Much of the information is standard no matter what sport you are in. The questionnaire is divided into four areas:

(1) Personal information,
(2) Family information,
(3) Academic information, and
(4) Athletic information (for one sport only).

The best way for me to explain what to include is to list it all. You can print out the list I've included, fill in your student-athlete information by hand, and then build your detailed questionnaire from that. This is a simple process, but explaining it may make it appear complex.

You can refer to the sample on the next page.

BASEBALL PROSPECT QUESTIONNAIRE

Today's Date: XX/XX/20XX   HS Graduation Date: 06/XX

Travis J. Fallon   **Ht:**   5'11"
1270 Lake Drive   **Wt:**   170 lbs.
San Luis Obispo, CA 93405
(805) 555-2383   E-mail: tfallon@myemail.com
Father: John Fallon   **Occupation:** Radio Station Manager   **Phone:** (805) 555-4848
College: *Indiana University (Played Varsity Baseball at Indiana Univ. 1976-78)*

Mother: Nancy Fallon   **Occupation:** Administrative Assistant   **Phone:** (805) 555-3121
College: *Miami of Ohio*

Currently living with: father and mother

ACADEMIC INFORMATION

High School: San Luis Obispo HS (Class of 20XX)   **Principal:**   David Harris
1350 Ross Blvd.   **AD:**   Tom Barry
San Luis Obispo, CA 93405   **Guidance Counselor:**   Jim Vellon
(805) 555-5773

High School GPA: 3.8/4.0   **Academic interest:** Graphic Design
Class Rank: 100 of 402   Will I apply for financial aid? Yes
PSAT: V: 490   M: 630   No. in family: 5   No. in college in 2017: 3
SAT: V: 500   M: 590   ACT: 24
Academic Honors: Golden State Exam Award: Math/Science/Spanish; Honor Roll; School Letter for Academic Excellence; 20XX Northern League Scholar Athlete; S Luis Obispo HS 20XX Scholar Athlete for 4.0 GPA in season.

BASEBALL INFORMATION

Pitcher and position player.

Primary Position: Pitcher   **Secondary Positions:** OF/1B   **Bats:** L **Throws:** R
Head HS Baseball Coach: Jim Thomas   Home/cell phone: (805) 555-4088
HS Pitching Coach: Alan Eastland   Home/cell phone: (805) 555-5408
20XX Summer Baseball Coach: Charlie Danielson   Home/cell phone: (805) 555-8899
20XX Summer Baseball Coach: Ron Sorland   Home/cell phone: (805) 555-1243

	G	ST	R	H	IP	K	BB	ERA	W	L
20XX HS Pitch Stats:	11	10	39	37	59.1	58	26	2.83	7	2
20XX HS Pitch Stats:	8	6	15	29	35.1	25	16	2.38	3	2
20XX Summer Pitch:	4	1	4	9	8.0	6	3	3.50	2	0

(mid-summer arm soreness— limited pitching—fully recovered for Fall season)
Pitches: Fast, curve, change   **Velocity:** 83 MPH   **Video?** Yes

	AB	H	R	BA	SB	BB	K
20XX HS Hitting Stats:	71	20	18	.282	1	10	12
20XX HS Hitting Stats:	62	20	9	.323	2	18	8
20XX Summer Hitting:	255	84	64	.329	7	32	58

Accomplishments: 20XX Team One West Regional selection: pitched two hitless shutout innings; Starting OF on 20XX High School CIF Championship Team; BA .329 with 255 official AB's on 2002 summer travel team, including 27 doubles and 4 triples; 2-0 summer record.
Top Players I have faced: Kyle Martin (20XX) Arroyo Grande HS; Brent Williams (20XX) Mission Prep

Here is what you will want your personal questionnaire to include:

Personal information:

- Today's date
- High School Graduation Date
- Name
- Address
- Phone number
- Email address
- Height
- Weight

Family information:

- Father's name
- Occupation
- Work phone number
- Home/cell phone number
- College he graduated from (if any)
- College athletic experience (if any)
- Mother's name
- Occupation
- Work phone number
- Home/cell phone number
- College she graduated from (if any)
- College athletic experience (if any)
- Currently living with (mother and father; mother; father, etc.)

Academic information:

- High school name and address
- Principal
- Athletic Director
- Guidance Counselor
- GPA
- Class rank (for instance: 42 of 351)

- PSAT   Math, Writing, Reading
- SAT   Math, Writing, Reading
- ACT
- Academic interest (possible majors)
- Will I apply for financial aid? (Yes or No)
- Number of people in family
- Number of children in college the year you will start
- Academic honors

Athletic Information:

This area will vary, of course, depending on the sport you are in. When you get to the statistics, you want to include the standard stats used for your sport. See Appendix A for sample sports to make sure you've covered the stat areas adequately.

- Primary position
- Secondary position(s)
- Indicate whether you are right-handed/footed or left-handed/footed, if applicable
- Head High School Coach
- Home/cell phone
- Secondary coach, if any (pitching, defense, goalie, etc.)
- Home/cell phone
- Summer or club coach
- Home/cell phone
- Stats (See Appendix A for headings, see example for format)
- Accomplishments
- Top players I have competed against (name and high school)

You Will Need the Questionnaire *FAST*

You should build this questionnaire quickly after you have sent out your first emails or letters. That's because within days, you may receive responses. The faster you can get back to the coaches, the better.

Feeling Overwhelmed?

Right now, you might feel overwhelmed, having to write your letter/email, your profile and your questionnaire. But, let me assure you, once these are done, the hardest work is behind you.

These three documents are the basis for most of the written communication you will make with the coaches.

NOTE: When you send your questionnaire, it's a good idea to also send your season schedule, whether it is your current high school or club team schedule.

Also, every time you enter a new season, send your schedule as an update to the coaches. This will give the coaches an opportunity to see you compete if they are in the vicinity where you are competing. You never know when they'll be nearby looking at prospects.

BUILD YOUR QUESTIONNAIRE

Key Points:

- Instead of completing every school's questionnaire, build your own, which incorporates all the information a coach will need to have.

- Build your questionnaire quickly after you send out your letters, because you will begin receiving responses from coaches in a few days.

- Send your upcoming season schedule, if you have it already, when you send your completed questionnaire.

Discuss It:

- Are you overwhelmed right now with the process, or are you doing ok? If you're overwhelmed, where do you need help?

- What are your college dreams?

Chapter Eight:

Key to Success: Track Your Communication

Gentlemen, start your engines. The volley of communication will now begin. You've sent out letters/emails and profiles to dozens of coaches, you're receiving questionnaire requests and you're completing online forms.

It can all get out of control if you don't adopt a good journaling and tracking system from the start. Besides the written communication, you may begin receiving phone calls, too, adding to the number of communications to keep track of.

You want to track dates of communications, who you wrote or talked with, and any notes you want to make about the interactions. Don't think you can get by with a stack of Post-It notes or a pile of scribbled papers. You will be interacting with multiple coaches and programs. If you aren't careful, they'll all begin to blur together.

I'm warning you in advance: you need a good, organized system to keep track of all the steps and interactions. It's the only way you'll survive.

Journal Your Interactions

The easiest way to do this is to keep a digital chart that you print out often. You can set this up as an Excel spreadsheet or Word Table, or something comparable. The point is to prepare to journal all the interactions with the dozens of coaches you'll be communicating with. Whichever method you feel most comfortable with, get it ready now.

You should set your chart up in "landscape" mode so you'll have more space for notes.

I recommend you create nine columns, with the following headings:

- School
- Coach
- Phone/email
- My interest level (None, low, medium, high)
- Sent letter and profile (Enter date)
- Sent questionnaire (Enter date)
- Sent video link (Enter date)
- Updates sent (Enter date and what you sent)
- Contact dates and notes

SCHOOL	COACH	PHONE/ EMAIL	MY INT LVL	SENT LTR & PROFL	COMPL QUEST	SENT VIDEO LINK	SENT UPDATES	CONTACT DATES AND NOTES
Air Force Academy	Reed Peters	719-333-7898 FAX 719-333-9267 Rp221@usafa.edu	High	7/15	7/25		9/10ff completing Congressional app	7/7 recvd letter-saw me at Team One 7/20 follow up ltr 8/4 phone call 8/14 phone call 7/10 process started for applying 8/25 recvd ph call asst. coach 9/15 Phone call from Head Coach Peters— classified them as Blue Chip 9/22 I called coach about getting forms to move to next level; coach called back 9/25 Dad called to get me moved to next level of app process 9/25 scheduled visit for 11/9-12
Biola University	John Verhoeven	562-944-0351 x5937 JV013@ Biola.edu	High	4/1	6/25	8/21	6/15 HS stats 8/21 summer stats	3/27 recvd ltr 8/21 wrote him a note asking for workout in fall and notifying about fall sked 8/22 Coach called about seeing us at Tourney labor Day wknd 8/29 Coach called Dad about seeing me this wknd; Practice Oct 16-Dec 8; best visit time last wknd Oct—can be accepted that day if paperwork filled out—more liberal at beginning; BB scholarships- 5 full tuitions, makes decisions late—Mar/Apr 9/3 met coach at Labor Day Tourn.; scholarships range from 1-10K; encouraged workout w/ team
Centenary	Ed McCann		Med	9/13	9/13			9/12 Coach McCann called—ref by Ritch Price; said he'd call weekly and send mat'fs; he is extremely interested 9/22 I left message to stay in touch 9/24 Coach called. Long conversation. Will pay for visit. Will be in Calif Oct. 7
Dartmouth College	Bob Whalen	603-646-2477 H- 603-643-6945	Low	6/25	7/7	8/21	8/21- summer stats	7/5 recvd letter 9/18 Ritch Price called Coach to recommend. Coach said he could probably get me in. 9/22 I called to stay in touch 9/24 Decided NO

You'll notice the "My interest level" column give you the option of indicating what your interest level is in the school.

You may be asking, "Why would I contact a school if I have no or low interest?" There are two reasons for scoring your interest level.

First, your interest level in particular schools changes as the process goes along.

Second, some schools may contact you first – even though they weren't on your list. You want to track these communications, too, as you may get interested as time goes along. Update this column regularly.

Be Prepared for Calls from Coaches

If a coach calls you, it usually means he or she has more than just a passing interest in you. Just as the coach wants to find out if you have an interest in the school, you want to find out what kind of interest the coach has in you.

The first call will center on that subject. I recommend telling the coach you have an interest and that you need to find out more about the school and program. Keep all your options open for as long as possible. Since you've probably already been communicating by mail or e-mail, the call is likely a follow-up to that.

Have your own questions ready. It is good to have a list of questions you want to ask the coaches. Print out the list and keep it with you, or have it on your phone. That way you take advantage of the opportunity to ask your questions.

If the coach calls when your parents are around, it is a good idea to put them on the phone so they can ask questions, too. You can even put your phone on speaker so they can participate in the conversation.

When our sons were being recruited, I took most of the calls and got to know the coaches. That's because we had a home phone. However, that's rare these days. Therefore, the student-athlete will have to make sure he or she brings the parents into the conversation.

NCAA rules dictate how often a coach can call, so get as much information as you can. Your parents may have some questions, too. Take a look at **Appendix B: What to Ask a Coach** for some guidance on good questions to ask.

This is where the tracking sheet comes into play. If you have specific questions for specific coaches, then write them on the sheet so you have the questions easily available.

Write everything down. Take notes as you talk with the coach. With the number of schools you'll be communicating with, you need to keep good written records. Transfer these notes into your tracking sheet before you forget the details.

Most of the time, it's not going to be convenient to write things down. All you've got is your phone. In that case, send yourself an email with the highlights of the call. Then enter the information into your spreadsheet later.

What Do You Say When You Talk with a Coach?

Engage in conversation with a coach. If you're an introvert like I am, I know that can be hard. That's why it's good to have your questions and conversation topics handy.

Here are some suggested conversation topics:

- Let the coach know how you are doing in your sport, if you are competing at the time.
- Ask your questions about the program, the school, the team, the coaching staff.
- Ask him what the team's needs are.
- What are the team's strengths and weaknesses?
- You can ask him about his coaching style and coaching philosophy.

Remember, just as much as he is recruiting you, you are recruiting a school. It is always good to have something to discuss.

At times, you will receive a call from a school you did not contact. They found out about you through a reference, perhaps through your high school coach. Or they saw you in competition.

The call might surprise you at first, but keep the lines of communication open even though you did not initiate the contact. You never know where it will take you.

If a coach leaves a voicemail on your cell, it is perfectly all right to call him or her back. In fact, the more you keep the communication going, the better. If you appear to lose interest in the school, they will lose interest in you and the calls will stop.

It's NOT your goal to see how many calls you can receive, but it is to keep as many options open as possible. I cannot overemphasize the importance of that.

TRACK YOUR COMMUNICATION

Key Points:

- Things can get out of control if you don't have a good tracking system for all the emails, letters, and phone calls.

- The best tracking tool is a chart that you complete as you go through the recruiting process.

- Have your questions for the coach ready in advance so you can ask them when he or she calls.

- See Appendix B for ideas for questions to ask a coach.

Discuss It:

- What are some questions I want to ask coaches when they call?

- Parent, what do you want to ask?

Chapter Nine:

Keeping a Coach's Interest

"The key to making the program work for you is to follow the most important rule of this system, which is "keep in contact with the coaches!" Sending out the updates is crucial!" --Donald, a Recruit-Me dad.

As an introduction to this chapter, watch my short two-minute video:

https://youtu.be/ZMt3xcvj1X0

You have interest from college coaches. They are emailing, writing, calling, texting or a combination of these. They are recruiting you.

That doesn't mean they will stay interested. If you don't continue the conversation, they will move on to other recruits and you'll get lost and forgotten.

How sad, since you've put in so much time and effort to get the coach's attention!

Keeping a coach's interest is a highly strategic part of the recruiting process.

Coaches prefer to recruit athletes that have expressed interest in their program ... and athletes that *continue* to express interest.

Don't believe the lie that coaches will keep coming after you based on your talent alone. **Talent + interest = a prime recruit.**

You need to continue communicating with the coaches. After a certain date, depending on your sport, they are permitted to call you, and some will. Although they are limited by how often they can call you, you are allowed to call them as often as you'd like.

Visit the NCAA website for the current contact chart, which lists each sport and the contact dates and windows.

Respond, Respond, Respond

Make sure you stay in touch with the coaches -- proactively. Remember: if you stop communicating with the coaches, they will assume you've lost interest.

Therefore, respond to every letter, e-mail or phone call, even if you don't have much interest in the school.

That's because you do not want to eliminate any schools until you're close to making your decision. You'll be surprised how many offers you thought would materialize that never do, and a school that was not at the top of your list moves up.

Send an Update After Every Season

One of the best ways you can show coaches you're still interested is by sending one-page updates at key intervals.

I'm reminded of one parent, Bob, who was diligent in keeping coaches interested in his daughter. He informed coaches of where her club and high school teams were playing by sending the schedules in advance.

After his daughter competed in some showcase tournaments, she started to get feedback from coaches. They heard from coaches ranging from D1 to D3.

To quote Bob, "Most of these contacts from coaches were from a result of us writing them and letting them know where she would play and keeping that line of communication open."

Take a lesson from Bob in how to keep the relationships alive.

My advice is that you should send an update at least at the end of each high school season and club season. It provides highlights of the season, updates your stats and shows the coaches that you are still interested.

And, as Bob discovered, including your upcoming schedule if you are going to compete on a club team in the offseason is a must.

How to Build a One-Page Update

The one-page update is another opportunity to highlight your successes and bring the coach current on your athletic and academic achievements.

You can email the update as an attached file. By this point in the communications process, you probably have some relationship with the coach. Therefore, e-mail is a great way for ongoing communication and updates.

I suggest using a narrative format for your update, with bullet points for each thought. Include things like:

- At the top: Your name, city, state
- Heading: Highlights for [Season]
- Current GPA (Coaches love to see success here)
- Academic honors
- Athletic highlights
- Athletic awards and achievements
- Stats from your latest season
- Other vital info on your achievements or competitiveness
- Immediate future plans
- Special moment
- Address and phone number at the bottom

Sending updates is the best way to show your continued interest and have the coaches update your file. Sending an update at the end of each season is the **minimum** you should do. You should use every opportunity to send out some kind of update whenever there is new information to communicate, such as:

- SAT or ACT test scores
- GPA update
- Academic or athletic honors
- Schedule for upcoming season

Of course, you won't always have a full sheet to fill, so you can send the information in an e-mail which simply says something like:

Dear Coach:

I just received my SAT scores and wanted to let you know so you can update my file. My scores were...

Thanks for your continued interest in me. I'm still interested in your program.

I will continue to update you on my athletics and academics.

**PLEASE ADD THIS
INFORMATION TO MY FILE**

TOMMY RICHARDS
San Luis Obispo, California

Class of 20XX
Bats: R Throws: R

Spring/Summer Highlights 20XX

- 4.1 cumulative GPA through Junior year at one of California's top high schools (Class rank 46 of 402). *Northern League* Scholar Athlete Award.

- Threw two hitless, shutout innings in *Team One West Regional* Showcase.

- Selected as one of only five 16-year-olds on 16-18 Summer travel team: San Luis Obispo Firestone Rangers, playing a 93-game schedule throughout Western States. (23-player roster). Team finished 5th in USABF World Series.

- .322 batting average for Summer travel team, and was one of only four pitchers who also played regularly as position players.

- 4-3 won-loss record for the Rangers.

- Resumed catching in final third of Summer season after full recovery from knee injury a year ago. Started several games at that position and could be team's #1 catcher this fall, in addition to pitching.

- Will play Fall ball with the San Luis Obispo Rangers for second consecutive year, competing against Junior Colleges and Scout teams.

- **Special moment**: My first game back in catcher's gear! I love catching as much as pitching.

1270 Ranch Road
San Luis Obispo, California 93405
Trichards5211@gmail.com
(805) 555-1212

SEND ONE-PAGE UPDATES

Key Points:

- Sending one-page updates tells the coach you are still interested in the school.

- Send an update at the end of each high school or club season. Send shorter updates when there is something significant to report to coaches.

- It is important to keep communicating with the coaches, or they will likely stop communicating with you.

Discuss It:

- Are there some new schools that I'm interested in now?

- Do I need to send an introductory letter/profile package to some other coaches?

Chapter Ten:

Choose the Right Camps and Showcases

Q: A lot of my friends are going to camps held at different colleges. Some are going to "showcases" where coaches show up to evaluate players. How important are these in getting recruited?

There is no substitute for a coach seeing you compete in person. That's when you'll get an honest evaluation and a good idea whether you will fit into the program.

Camps, showcases, combines and recruiting tournaments **can** be excellent opportunities, but you can go broke attending them. You have to be selective, because they will run you anywhere from $300-$750 each, plus travel and expenses. You can't afford too many at that price.

Camps Can Be Good for Instruction and Exposure

Let's talk about camps first. These are good recruiting tools for some programs, but are just fundraisers for most. In many camps, you will pick up some good instruction. However, for the price, that's not your primary reason for attending. You want to show the coaches your talent and you might get to know them on a personal level, too. If you end up going to their school, that helps.

Camps can last from one day to one week. At the multiple day camps, there are often coaches from several schools there as instructors to handle the large number of athletes. That's good because you are seen by schools you may not have known anything about. You get to know coaches, and your interest level may shift to a school you may not have had an interest in. In addition, coaches from different levels are there, which also widens the opportunities.

A camp helps you see how well you compete against better competition than you may face during the season. In most cases, the athletes who show up for the camps are usually from all over the country or region.

At a camp, there will be instruction time and competition. There is also a lot of interaction with coaches, which is far better than a weekly phone call or letter. You can get to know a lot about the coach, such as his or her abilities, character and coaching style.

I recommend only going to a camp at the schools where you are very interested in attending. Or a camp where the coach from a school you are interested in will be instructing. An exception would be to attend a camp where there are many coaches, so you can get a lot of exposure. You must be selective, though, because this is an expensive process.

Showcases Allow More Coaches to See You

Showcases and combines are supposedly open only to "select" athletes. You have to be recommended, so they say, but some of the showcases work off mailing lists and will accept non-recommended athletes.

My sons attended a showcase and that is where they were spotted by the coach of one of the schools where they were recruited and where they attended. So, for them, it was a good move.

However, showcases do not allow that much individual exposure because there are so many athletes there. For instance, at a baseball showcase, you may get 15 batting practice pitches, run the 60, take infield practice, and play in a couple of scrimmages (with few at bats). All this for a very steep cost, with hardly enough exposure to give coaches a chance to look at you in depth.

The advantage of a showcase is that there are a lot of coaches there, which is an excellent situation.

Let Coaches Know You'll Be There

If you are interested in a particular school, and you know the coach will be at the showcase, alert him or her in advance so you can be "looked at" during the showcase.

The NCAA recruiting rules don't allow coaches to talk with you at the showcases – but they **can** look. You'll see them making notes on their clipboard or iPad or laptop. If you let them know in advance, your name will already be on their list.

One More Thing

Keep in mind that another great way to get seen by coaches of schools you're interested in is to let them know when you will be competing in their area. And that's free.

CHOOSE THE RIGHT CAMPS AND SHOWCASES

Key Points:

- Be selective. Camps and showcases are expensive.

- When choosing a camp, go to ones at schools that are on your list, or to ones where coaches from your list will be attending.

- Showcases allow you to be seen by many coaches in one place.

Discuss It:

- What camps or showcases am I interested in?

- What other schools do I want to look at for camps?

- What is our budget for camps and showcases?

Chapter Eleven:

Register With the NCAA and NAIA Eligibility Centers

Before you will be considered as a student-athlete candidate, you must register with the NCAA and NAIA Eligibility Centers. The Eligibility Center will validate your transcripts, test scores, and proof of graduation (once that happens) to certify that you have met the Core Course requirements and that your GPA, SAT and ACT scores meet the minimum qualifications for incoming freshmen student-athletes.

Schools considering you as a student-athlete will request your certification from the Eligibility Center. This will allow you to receive an athletic scholarship or to practice or compete at the Division I or II levels.

Check the Core Class Requirements

In preparation for this, you should check with your high school counselor no later than the **first semester of your sophomore year** to make sure you will meet the Core Course requirements by the time you graduate. Once you and your counselor have mapped out the courses to meet these requirements, you should not change your class schedule without first determining whether your NCAA or NAIA eligibility will be affected.

When to Register

The best time to register with the Eligibility Centers is at the **beginning of your junior year**. To register with the Center, visit the website and complete the online registration and create an account. There is a fee, but you can receive a fee waiver if you have also received an SAT or ACT fee waiver. By registering, you authorize each high school you have attended to send the Center your transcript, test scores, proof of graduation (once it occurs) and other necessary academic information. It also authorizes the Center to send your academic information to all colleges that request your eligibility status.

Register at:

http://eligibilitycenter.org

https://www.playnaia.org/eligibility-center

You can always check your status with the Center online.

For complete details about the Eligibility Centers, go to their websites, or see the details in the online version of the *Guide for the College-Bound Student-Athlete*. The web address to download the NCAA Guide is:

http://www.ncaapublications.com/productdownloads/CBSA17.pdf

This is the 2016-17 edition. Subsequent years can be downloaded as they are released. Substitute the year you are looking for in place of "CBSA17" in the web address.

The NAIA Guide can be downloaded at:

http://www.naia.org/fls/27900/1NAIA/membership/NAIA_Guide fortheCollegeBoundStudent.pdf?DB_OEM_ID=27900

(Because links change often, you may find that a link included in this book is broken. It was live at the time of publication. However, you can get the correct link by doing a Google Search).

REGISTER WITH THE NCAA AND NAIA ELIGIBILITY CENTERS

Key Points:

- You must register with the NCAA and NAIA Eligibility Centers to be considered a prospective student-athlete by each of the associations.

- You should plan with your counselor no later than first semester of your sophomore year to assure that you've met your Core Course requirements by the time you graduate.

- You should register with the Center at the beginning of your junior year.

Discuss It:

- Do I need to make any changes in my planned courses to meet the Core Course requirements?

- When will I be registering with the Eligibility Centers?

Chapter Twelve:

Parent-Athlete Teamwork

Larry and his daughter worked for three years at the recruiting process. As he put it, "lots of letters, emails, follow-ups, camps, showcase games, and getting up the nerve to make phone calls."

There were ups and downs along the way, but they stuck with it. Together. While Larry was doing his part, his daughter was doing her part.

She ultimately made her dream come true by being persistent in the recruiting process and working hard at softball and at her school work. And it resulted in an athletic scholarship.

Larry said his daughter couldn't be happier with her decision. He told me that it will be fun for her to play out her remaining high school and travel ball seasons knowing she will be playing softball and attending the school of her choice, a D1 university.

The recruiting journey is one that you should take as a family, if at all possible. Parents have an important role, as does the student-athlete.

Take a couple minutes and watch this very short video where I share two important words about recruiting:

https://youtu.be/zvwR2tqqOFY

This is not a sprint, but a marathon, and you will need each other for encouragement, support and sharing the workload.

When Patricia went through the Recruit-Me steps with her daughter, Patricia was the one that read the manual and helped her daughter put her package together.

Then her daughter took over the emails, the updates and the phone calls to coaches. "That's important because it shows how much the student-athlete really wants it," said Patricia. "My daughter is a senior in high school now and was recruited early last year to play lacrosse for a top DI college."

While it may not be possible for the student-athlete to take over all the work, you should divide the responsibilities.

If you are a student-athlete, here are the things you should focus on:

1. **Your academics**. I can't tell you how important this is. You can literally eliminate yourself from a scholarship opportunity by getting into grade trouble. However, you can lift yourself above other scholarship prospects by excelling in academics. Do the best job you can. That's all anyone can ask.

2. **Become a better athlete**. The more skilled you become, the greater your chances of being noticed and getting a scholarship. There's no doubt about it, this is a competitive field. Other athletes in your sport are working on getting better, and you need to stay ahead of as many of them as possible.

   The amount of work you put into improving will indicate how serious you are about competing past high school. Although you can't do all of the things I will list, you can pick one or two: attend instructional camps, take lessons, watch instructional videos, video your performance and study it, find someone who will mentor you in your sport. When it stops being fun, then it is probably time to give up the sport and pursue other interests.

3. **Communicate with coaches.** Be sure to write and call coaches. Provide coaches with updates after every season. Write or call back if they write or call you. If you stop communicating with them, they will assume you are no longer interested. You want to keep your options open until you are certain you are

not interested in that school. Usually that will come in the final months before you make your decision.

4. **Ask a parent or an adult mentor to help you go through this process.** You need someone on your team. Preferably, a parent. However, if that is not possible, then find someone who can help you succeed. It is too tough and too long to go through this yourself. And you will need someone you can ask advice and actually help you do some of the letter writing and tracking communications.

As for parents:

1. **Be an encourager.** Your son or daughter will need this. There will be a lot of ups and downs. He or she will be pursued by some coaches and rejected by others. You'll have to help your child keep a positive attitude and move forward.

2. **Handle the admin.** Take the leadership in drafting the introductory emails, profiles and questionnaires. Don't do all the work yourself, but work as a team with your son or daughter. With all the communications to so many coaches, your child cannot do it all and still compete athletically and academically. And, over time, you will have to keep a good record of the communications with the coaches.

3. **Discuss the process with your son or daughter.** Find out what is going through his or her mind along the way. Get an idea of his or her interest in certain schools. Work through it together as you narrow down your choices.

If you work together as a team, each carrying out his or her role, the whole process will be less stressful.

PARENT-ATHLETE TEAMWORK

Key Points:

- The student-athlete's focus should be on academics, improving athletically, and communicating with the coaches.

- The parent's focus should be on encouraging your son or daughter and handling the paperwork.

Discuss It:

- How can we work most effectively as a team on this project?

NOTE: Parent-Athlete teamwork starts with learning the recruiting process together. My six-module video course may help keep you on the same page as you experience the teaching together. Find out more at www.AthleticScholarshipUniversity.com

Chapter Thirteen:
International Students

NCAA

If you are a foreign student, you are able to receive an athletic scholarship at U.S. colleges and universities, just as U.S. students are. However, first you must be academically eligible. The minimum required standards will vary depending on your country.

Also, if you are not currently enrolled in a college or university in your country or in the U.S., you will need a minimum score on the SAT or the ACT. Foreign students MUST take the SAT or the ACT. Other tests, such as the TOEFL or the TWSE, are not acceptable.

For more information on the SAT, please contact Educational Testing Service or College Board Online. For information on the ACT, please contact www.act.org.

The NCAA website provides all the information you need to determine your eligibility and get details on international student-athletes. Go to:

http://www.ncaa.org/student-athletes/future/international-student-athletes

If you are currently enrolled (or have previously been enrolled) as a full-time student at a university in a foreign country, you will be considered a transfer student (not an incoming freshman) upon enrolling at a NCAA university. Please see the NCAA Transfer Guide for more information on your eligibility. Go to:

http://www.ncaapublications.com/productdownloads/TGONLINE2014.pdf

NAIA

An incoming international freshman student must meet the same requirements required of a domestic freshman student. If high school GPA and class ranking cannot be determined, then the international student can be determined eligible by meeting the NAIA institution's admission criteria for international students and by meeting the following NAIA criteria:

1. A minimum score of 18 on the ACT or 860 on the SAT as mandated under item 2(a).

2. Meet the entering freshman requirements as defined for students from each country in the most current Guide to International Academic Standards for Athletics Eligibility (GIAS on freshman form) published by the NCAA using AACRAO guidelines.

Chapter Fourteen:

Junior Colleges

Sometimes student-athletes fall short of the academic requirements of the 4-year schools at which they'd like to compete. If their grades keep them out of the 4-year schools, I recommend they consider attending a junior college while they work on raising their grades, and that they continue to play their sport while there.

It's not well-known that scholarships are available at *some* junior colleges for some sports. However, junior college scholarships are not as plentiful as at 4-year schools.

So whether you are pursuing a junior college scholarship or just looking for the best place to compete, the Recruit-Me System can help you. Your steps of action are still the same, whether you are seeking to be recruited by 4-year schools or 2-year schools.

The governing body is the National Junior College

Athletic Association (NJCAA) and their website is www.njcaa.org. Member colleges are accredited two-year institutions.

The NJCAA is comprised of three divisions, with scholarships offered only at the Division I and II levels. Division I colleges may offer full scholarships, and Division II may offer partial scholarships (tuition or fees and books).

Note: Students who attend a junior college with the intention of transferring to a four-year college (perhaps with an athletic scholarship) must be certain that their course credits will transfer, as not all will.

Chapter Fifteen:

Home Schooled Students

NCAA

Students who were home schooled for any part of high school must register with the NCAA Eligibility Center. They will process all home-school certifications. This means that you do not have go through this process on a school-by-school basis. Once certified, a home school student is eligible to compete in the NCAA.

Begin by going to the Eligibility Center website at www.eligibilitycenter.org and follow the prompts to register.

You must complete all the following steps for the NCAA Eligibility Center to certify you as eligible to play NCAA sports:

- Register with the NCAA Eligibility Center at eligibilitycenter.org.
- Pay your registration fee.
- Register to take the ACT or SAT and submit your scores directly to the NCAA with code 9999. Test scores on transcripts or Student Score Reports are not used by the NCAA Eligibility Center.
- Submit an official transcript for each high school or academic program you attended.
- Submit proof of high school graduation with a specific graduation date.
- Submit a signed statement of who managed the home school program (e.g., who taught and evaluated the coursework, awarded grades and issued credit); and a signed statement that home schooling was conducted in accordance with state laws..
- Submit core-course worksheets for English, math, natural or physical science, social science, foreign language, comparative religion or philosophy classes.

[Source: NCAA website]

It is best to register at the beginning of your junior year of high school. All of the above documents must be submitted to be considered for certification. Some college coaches may be concerned that you will not qualify for certification, so it is advised that you submit your SAT and ACT scores to the coaches, as well as your transcript to date.

For more details on home school qualifications, go to the NCAA website at:

http://ncaa.org/student-athletes/future/home-school-students

NAIA

Home schooled students must meet entering freshmen requirements, though the criteria for meeting those requirements have been adapted to fit the distinctive high school experience.

The eligibility of home schooled students follows one of two pathways:

Test scores only

- Home school students who meet the minimum NAIA home school ACT or SAT test score are considered to have met the freshman eligibility requirement.
- 20 on the ACT** or
- 950 on the SAT (Critical Reading and Math), if taken before March 2016
- 1030 on the SAT (Evidence-Based Reading and Writing + Math), if taken in March 2016 or after.*

Students who earn below the required 1030 and at or above the previous 950 minimum on exams taken March 2016 and beyond who will compete in the 2016-17 academic year can meet an exception to the 1030 SAT minimum.

** *Students who earn below the required 20 and at or above an 18 on exams taken March 2016 and beyond who will compete in the 2016-17 academic year can meet an exception to the 20 ACT minimum.*

- A final home school transcript must be sent to the NAIA Eligibility Center, but GPA is not used to determine eligibility.
- Class rank is not applicable.

OR

111

Request Committee Review

- Students achieving a minimum test score of 18 on the ACT or 860 on the SAT for tests taken prior to March 2016 and 940 for test taken March 2016 and beyond will be reviewed on the individual's unique academic history. (Sending test scores)
- An NAIA school may request an exceptional ruling. The student will go to the Home School Advisory Committee and NAIA National Eligibility Committee for review and a determination.
- Students will still need to submit transcripts and test scores to the NAIA Eligibility Center before the student can be reviewed by the NEC.

[Source: NAIA website]

Visit https://www.playnaia.org/page/HomeSchoolGED.php for the most up-to-date details.

Chapter Sixteen:

The Importance of Your Academics

*"I can't emphasize enough how much coaches value having a player that is also very strong academically. It makes their job as coaches so much easier because no matter how good you are, you're no help to the team if you're failing out of school, and they do **not** want to spend their time wondering whether you'll be academically eligible to play." -G.M., a Recruit-Me Dad*

You may be one of the best athletes in the area, but if you do not perform in the classroom, you will disqualify yourself from many schools. The coach won't even look at you if you fall well below the standards at his college or university. He'd be wasting his time trying to recruit someone he couldn't get admitted because of bad grades or a student-athlete who is not likely to last at the school.

Watch this video as I share how your academics can give you an edge in recruiting:

https://youtu.be/Uh6VN_3c5Eo

The dad I quoted told me that his son received a 50% athletic scholarship to an ACC school. It was increased to 70% in his junior year "due to his success on the field and his high academic standing."

To increase your chances of an athletic scholarship, do yourself a favor: be a first-class student. Do your best. I think you know in your heart what "best" means for you. **Excel in the classroom just as you excel as an athlete, and you will open up huge opportunities.** With good grades and good SAT scores, you will beat out competitors with lesser grades and scores.

As an athlete, you have extra time pressures that most students don't have to face. You have practices, personal workouts, road trips and competitions that cut into your time available for study. If you also have a job, your study time is very restricted.

But you also have an advantage over many other students. To rise to the level you've attained as a top athlete, you've already learned to **discipline** yourself, to follow a plan, and to press on even when you don't really want to. That's one of your advantages.

Now let me give you an additional advantage: **a crash course on how to study, write reports, and take tests most effectively.** Most students never think through their game plan on studying, writing, or even test-taking. They just assume that they know how it all works, since they've been in school since their earliest memories. They're probably wrong. They don't realize that there's a way to significantly increase their performance academically, while requiring less time studying. That's what I'm going to share with you now.

It's a report by Dr. Bob Kizlik, a comprehensive "tip sheet" on how to excel academically. It's quick and to the point. There's no fluff in there. Read, understand and take these suggestions to heart, and your grades will get better while your time spent studying will decrease.

Sound good? Then let me recommend this little guide written by educator Dr. Bob Kizlik. Visit his website at:

www.adprima.com/studyout.htm

THE IMPORTANCE OF YOUR ACADEMICS

Key Points:

- Coaches won't consider you, no matter how good you are, if your academics fall well below the standards for their school.

- When you excel in the classroom, you open up possibilities and you have an advantage over other student-athletes competing for the same scholarship.

Discuss It:

- How do you feel about your current academic situation and your grades? Parent, how do you feel?

- If necessary, what can be done to improve? Are there any study habits that could be better?

- What are your academic goals?

Chapter Seventeen:

Make Your School Choice Wisely

"I started with Kathleen my golfer when she was a sophomore, followed your program, and she received an offer for a full scholarship the first day that coaches could contact her. It was awesome! We started with 40 schools to contact, had it down to about 20 this past spring/summer, and we got the perfect deal."

--Bob

There is no absolute formula for choosing your school. You can walk through the process I've explained, but it will ultimately come down to your choice. You will have to weigh and evaluate a lot of factors and variables.

You might go through some tense times, there may be some heated conversations between parent and student-athlete, you'll have to deal with pressure from coaches, financial issues will arise, and the list goes on.

But, as Bob experienced with his daughter, Kathleen, if you follow through on the steps you've learned in this book, you'll have the opportunity to make a choice.

What it comes down to, above all, is that you find the school that is *the best fit*. There are a number of elements to consider.

Below is a checklist I've put together to help make the choice easier as you come down to the end:

- ✓ Net cost comparison. Take the total cost of the school and subtract all the financial aid offered.

- ✓ Scholarship offer. If the school does offer athletic scholarships, how good is the offer you have received? This could be an indication of the coach's commitment to you.

- ✓ Academic quality of the school

- ✓ Academic match: does the school offer majors in your areas of interest?

- ✓ Quality of the athletic program. Grade it from A to F

- ✓ Coaching staff: coaching ability, integrity, character, reputation

- ✓ Coach's interest level in you. How much of an effort did the coach make in the recruiting process? Evaluate his or her interest level in you. (Consider: How often does he or she call you? Were you offered an official visit? Where does he or she say you will fit into the program?)

- ✓ Potential for becoming a better athlete in the program

✓ Potential for earning a starting position within the first two years (you want to go where you can compete)

✓ My overall impression. Consider all the "feeling" factors: how much did you enjoy the school when you visited, talked with the coaches, players, did you like the area, etc.?

Add other factors that are important to you. Then build a "report card" to help in the decision-making process. Here's a sample:

School Report Card	School 1	School 2	School 3	School 4	School 5	School 6
Net cost after all financial aid	11,000	12,000	7,000	8,500	6,000	9,000
Athletic scholarship offer	Books/ fees	Room/ board	½ tuition	None	80%	Tuition
Academic quality	A	B	B+	A	B	B
Academic match	A	A	A	C	C	B
Quality of program	A	B	B	C	A-	B+
Coaching staff	A	B	B	B	B-	C
Coach's interest level in me	B	B	A	A	C	C+
Potential for my improvement	A	B	C	A	B	B
Potential to start in 1-2 years	C	B	A	A	C	B
Overall impression	B+	B	A-	C	B	B

A report card like this won't make the decision for you, but it will help you organize your thoughts and priorities so the best decision becomes more obvious.

MAKE YOUR FINAL SCHOOL CHOICE WISELY

Key Points:

- There is no absolute formula for choosing the right school.

- A checklist can help you develop a "report card" for each school. This will also help you make a more objective decision.

Discuss It:

- What schools are your top choices right now and why?

- Parent, what do you think about those choices?

Chapter Eighteen:

Advice From Recruit-Me Families

How can you maximize what you've learned in this book? The parent comments in this chapter are arranged by topic. I've included their stories in appropriate chapters in this book, but I thought it would be helpful to include them all here for quick reference as you take on the recruiting process.

Hear it from other Recruit-Me families as they share their experiences and what they have found worked for them. Each family has gone through the Recruit-Me steps. I hope this will help you focus on things that will make a difference as you continue your journey.

Parent-Athlete Teamwork

Your publication was a tremendous tool to use when my daughter was going through the recruiting process last year. It explained very clearly what needed to be done, when and what to expect through the whole process. I'm the one that read the manual and helped my daughter put her package together but then she took over and did everything that needed to be done. She took over the emails, the updates and the phone calls to coaches. That's important because it shows how much the student-athlete really wants it. My daughter is a senior in high school now and was recruited early last year to play lacrosse for a top DI college. – Patricia

Control of the Recruiting Process

My daughter is a basketball player currently in her junior year and is excited about having coaches write, e-mail and come see her play. She is still a long way from landing a scholarship at a school she wants to attend but without Recruit-Me she wouldn't even be considered. Yes, you do the work but it's worth it in the end because you have total control and focus on your son or daughter, and do not leave it up to someone who is looking after several interests. –Bob

Time and Effort

As a parent and a prospective student-athlete you must be willing to put in the time and effort to receive your reward. A college scholarship is the prize and we intend on continuing to use the system. I have made contact with over 15 schools and received responses from each with the exception of one within one week. We look forward to the day when we can say that a scholarship has been offered and accepted. –Chris

Maintaining Contact

You showed us how to present our son to prospective college coaches. The key to making the program work for you is to follow the most important rule of this system, which is "Keep in contact with the coaches!" Sending out the updates is crucial! –Donald

Covering all the bases

The main benefits for us was that we were fully prepared with Mike's recruiting necessities all in place, including Eligibility Center registration, player packet with profile, cover letter, video. The tips and important background information on recruiting and eligibility rules we learned was so priceless. –Michael

Hard work

You have to do the work yourself. The thought is that your club coach or high school coach will help promote you to the schools you want to attend. Not always true. If that school doesn't fit his expectations of where you fit in or where they want you to go, they might not be providing your schools with the type of feedback you would want them to hear. I've seen it first-hand. You (player and parents) select what's best for you. You have to do the work. Don't leave it up to the coaches. –Scott

Keeping Coaches up to Date

We had informed the coaches of where her club team was playing and when the high school season started with the schedules of both. After playing in some the "Showcase Tournaments" we started to get feedback from some coaches. We had broken down our selections to 5 Div. 1, 5 Div. 2 and 5 Div. 3 teams. We got feedback from 3 Div. 1's, 4 Div. 2's and 5 Div. 3 teams. Most of these contacts from the coaches were from a result of us writing them and letting them know where she would play and keeping that line of communication open. –Bob

Being Proactive

We have managed to catch interest in a lot of schools. Being proactive is the way to get noticed. He has had 2 unofficial visit requests and continues to get letters from many schools. My son can now focus on grades and his performance. He has managed to increase his GPA and his performance on the field! That is what he should be doing. This also gives me something to do besides sitting and waiting for something to happen. I would recommend Recruit-Me to any parent who is truly interested in providing all opportunities for their child to succeed. –Jeff

Making a Lot of Contacts

I purchased Recruit-Me after my son's sophomore year and immediately read the information and began following the process. We sent out 55 introductory

packets and began receiving letters and emails within a week. He has gotten 20 letters of interest and the correspondence continues to flow in. We will continue to follow the process throughout his last two years in High School and we expect to gain a scholarship. The process has opened the doors and has him on the radar of coaches. –Todd

Marketing Yourself

We started late in finding opportunities for my daughter looking to continue playing volleyball in college. We took your recommendations and started the process of creating the materials she would need to market herself to prospective coaches. Your system work wonderful as she had many contacts and eventually settled on a school with the high academic standards she was looking for as well as a full athletic scholarship at a D1 institution. –William

Final Words

Dear Sports Family,

This book has led you through the mechanics of the recruiting process, but it would be impossible to cover all the dynamics in a short time like this. You have the tools and teaching necessary to wade through the recruiting waters. If you follow the steps you've learned, you will do fine.

I want to remind you: there is no substitute for good grades and quality performance. That's what it will eventually come down to.

One of the most challenging things during this scholarship search process will be assessing your abilities against those with whom you are competing for a scholarship. You may be a star at your school or in your league, but you need to find out how that matches up with other student-athletes around the country. Many of them are stars, too.

You will need to come to terms with your abilities early on, and target the schools where you have the best chance of competing and receiving a scholarship. Be candid with coaches who are evaluating you. Ask them what they think of your talent. Your feelings might be hurt in some cases, or in other cases you may be surprised to find that have underestimated your talent. But this is vital information for you to have. You want to make sure you are targeting the right schools, and a big factor is your talent level.

When you have a pretty realistic assessment of your abilities, I recommend shooting for a few schools above your level (in order to challenge you), a few below (so you have something to fall back on) and the rest right in the ballpark.

126

Thanks for letting me help you. I've given you the framework, the mechanics, and the how-to guidance. Now do it!

You'll be greatly rewarded for your time and discipline. Your success is my success. I am here to help you succeed. So, don't go through this alone. Please keep in contact with me, because I want to help.

Jon Fugler, CEO
Recruit-Me
jon@recruit-me.com

Colorado Springs, CO

Appendix A:

Important Stats

These are the most important stats for several sports. This is what you will be including on your questionnaire. You should include only Varsity High School and club stats. If your sport is not listed, review the college stats from a team in your sport. Set up your stat headings accordingly.

SOFTBALL AND BASEBALL: POSITION PLAYERS

YR	AVG	GP	GS	AB	R	H	2B	3B	HR	RBI	BB	SO	SB	ATT	PO	A	E	%

SOFTBALL AND BASEBALL: PITCHERS

YR	ERA	W	L	APP	GS	CG	SHO	SV	IP	H	R	ER	BB	SO		

SOCCER: POSITION PLAYERS

YR	GP	GS	G	A	PTS	SHOTS	%					

SOCCER: GOALIE

YR	GP	GS	MIN	GA	AVG	SV	PCT	W	L	T	SHO				

BASKETBALL:

YR	GP	GS	FG	FGA	PCT	3FG	3FGA	PCT	FT	FTA	PCT	REB	PTS	AVG

FOOTBALL: RUSHING

YR	GP	ATT	YDS	AVG	TD	LONG								

FOOTBALL: QUARTERBACK

YR	GP	ATT	COMP	INT	PCT	YDS	TD	AVG/GM					

FOOTBALL: PASS RECEIVING

YR	GP	NO	YDS	TD	AVG/GM								

FOOTBALL: DEFENSE

YR	GP	SOLO	ASST	TOT	SACKS	INT		

FOOTBALL: KICKING

YR	NO. PUNTS	YDS	AVG	PAT ATT	PAT MADE	PCT		

FOOTBALL: KICK AND INTERCEPTION RETURNS

YR	PUNT RET	YDS	AVG	TD	LNG	KO RET	YDS	AVG	TD	LONG	INT RET	YDS	AVG	TD	LNG

129

Appendix B:

What to Ask a Coach

You're going to be talking with dozens of coaches, each of whom will want to put his or her institution and program in the best light to attract you. Here are some good questions on athletics and academics that will be of help as you talk with them. They will allow you to learn what you need to know about his athletic program and his school.

Athletics

Describe your coaching style.
All coaches have different coaching styles and use different techniques for motivation and discipline. It is to your benefit to ask this question to determine whether your learning style and the coach's style would be a good fit.

What are your expectations for the upcoming year?
Obviously, all coaches would like to see their programs succeed each year. By asking this question, you will learn the goals and objectives the coach has set forth to reach the final destination – a successful season.

Describe the walk-on process and the scholarship program.
You will learn how the coach handles his/her walk-ons. Each coach and institution treats walk-ons differently. Also, the scholarship programs will vary to some degree.

What role will I play on your team?
Many coaches will already have an idea of how they would like to utilize certain recruits. You will be able to find out where the coach sees you fitting in on his/her team and why.

What demands does this sport require physically and what time is required?
It is important to know the physical demands that will be placed on you during your tenure as an athlete. Also, you need to know how much time is spent with this sport so you may manage your study time wisely.

Academics

How strong is my degree program?
There are some institutions that have stronger programs than others. There are also those institutions that specialize in specific degree programs.

Does this major mix well with athletics?
Some majors are more time consuming than others and may require labs or mandatory work outside of class hours. You need to know the demands that will be placed on you within your major, to know if you are spreading yourself to thin through participating in athletics.

What is your view on academics?
Many coaches have different thoughts regarding academics. It is important to know that the coach's philosophy on academics will compliment yours.

131

What percentage of athletes graduates in four years?
This will tell you about a coach's commitment to academics. Also, the team grade point average is a good indicator of academic commitment.

College Life

What is a typical day for a student-athlete?
You will learn a typical schedule that will include courses, practices, meal times, study times, etc. This will give you insight as to how to manage your time and assist you with needed adjustments.

What does the institution's services entail?
You will be informed of any study hall hours that may be required of you during your tenure. Also, this is a good time to ask about the availability of tutors.

What is the average class size?
You will learn what type of attention you will be receiving as a student. Some larger institutions have large classes that tend to be taught by teaching assistants.

How would you describe the residence halls/campus housing and will I be required to live in campus housing as a student-athlete?
Sometimes student-athlete housing is provided and included in the scholarship you are allotted. It is important to know this before enrolling with the institution. Also, coaches and other institutional faculty have a better idea of what the residence halls are like and where they are located on campus.

Financial Aid

What is the length of my scholarship and what type of scholarship is it?

Most institutional scholarships are for only one year. Also, there are some scholarships that cover just tuition (or housing, or books) and others that cover housing, books, tuition, or full-ride scholarships.

Is there financial aid available for summer school?

Some athletes prefer to simply take the necessary course hours to be eligible to play during the season. This could leave you with several credit hours that you may wish to pick up during the summer. However, you may need financial assistance in the summer, so ask whether or not your financial aid packages cover summer expenses.

Describe the different financial aid packages.

It is important to know what your athletic scholarship entails. Also, it is important to know if you can supplement your athletic scholarship with other financial aid packages the institutions offers.

If I get seriously injured and I am unable to participate, what will happen to my scholarship?

Institutions are not obligated to offer scholarships or financial aid past the term of the agreement. It is important to know what the institution's commitment to injured athletes is.

Appendix C:

Frequently Asked Recruiting Questions

Although this book is a complete playbook, I still receive a lot of further questions from student-athletes and parents.

Once you begin the recruiting process yourself, you will find this Q & A section helpful. You may also have questions of your own, so you'll be able to identify with some of these.

If you have further questions, please e-mail me at jon@recruit-me.com and I will do my best to answer you promptly

Q: Do college coaches typically call the student-athlete or do they go through their high school coach, and which call carries more weight?

A: Coaches should initially contact the student, although many do some checking with your high school coaches. Their first sign of interest comes when they ask you to complete their questionnaire or request a video link. The first contact is **not** usually by phone. I would encourage you, though, to call the coaches if they have not responded within three weeks after you send the initial letter/email and profile. You can call them at any time and you can find out a lot of information that way. Taking the initiative is important.

Q: I play varsity doubles and have received all-state for 2 years, but it seems very hard to get noticed at the regional/national level in doubles. Any suggestions?

A: Your struggle is not an uncommon problem for most high school athletes. Even talented ones like yourself get overlooked. Most colleges' recruiting budgets are limited, and the coaches cannot get out to see that many players. They rely on tournaments, showcases and camps to see large numbers of players at once. Only for exceptional prospects will a coach normally travel to see an individual game or match.

For these reasons, it is extremely important that you take the initiative to let college coaches know about you. Be aggressive in pursuing the schools where you have an interest. Once you make contact with the coaches, you open the door for continued contact. They will write back if they see that you have the tools to play on their team. Your letter, player profile, completed questionnaire, video (if they ask for one), and regular updates are those tools.

If you sit back and wait for coaches to find you, it is likely not going to happen. That's the mistake most parents and athletes make. You'll miss the boat, because other athletes with your abilities (and less ability) are getting in line ahead of you by contacting the schools.

Q: What kind of grades in high school are acceptable in order to receive an athletic scholarship?

A: I cannot tell you how important it is to keep your grades up. If you cannot get into the school, the coach cannot get you on the team. The NCAA has standards for grades in order to be eligible for Intercollegiate Athletics, and they differ by division.

Keep in mind, though, that these are only NCAA minimum standards. The schools you are pursuing could be much higher.

Q: *My son did not receive a baseball scholarship, but wants to continue to play in college. Is it worth it, or is it only the scholarship kids that get to play?*

A: Your son can definitely continue to play baseball even if he does not receive a scholarship.   I did it myself. The coach may not see his talent until he gets there and tries out for the team. So much can happen during the course of the year. Players come and go, some do poorly while others bloom at some point during the year. If he makes the team, tell him to hang in there. Playing on the college level is a lot different, and he will have to determine how far he wants to go and how long he wants to play.

Q: *My son, Samuel, is a basketball lover who plays the game excellently. He is a freshman now. We are doing all that we can to prepare him for the next level of basketball through various camps, etc. What help and guidance can you give?*

A: First of all, let me say that I am happy that you are starting early in his high school career to prepare him for the recruiting process. Many parents and athletes wait until it is dangerously late. I recommend starting no later than the junior year, but even earlier is better.

Without overloading you with details, here are a few things I would recommend to your son:

1. Samuel, keep your grades up. If you don't have the grades, you will eliminate yourself from many colleges. That's one of the biggest things that keeps student-athletes from being recruited. If you don't meet the school's academic standards, the coach can't touch you.

2. Choose your camps carefully. As you know, camps are expensive. Choose the ones that have good reputations and will have a lot of quality colleges represented. As a family, once you narrow down your college choices, probably after your sophomore or junior year, consider attending a camp at one of your top choices.

3. Contact schools of interest now. Write your initial letter or email, just so the coaches can see your interest. They are not allowed to contact you as a freshman except to send questionnaires, camp information, NCAA materials and nonathletic publications. They can start a file on you. Continue to send them updates after each season.

I hope that helps in these early stages.

Q: My daughter's list of "best schools for her future" are very competitive (D-I); does your system help her even to have a chance at one of them? She'll be a senior, is not too late to start the process now. She is a great student and athlete.

A: You want to have as many options as possible, so you should divide your prospective schools into three categories: (1) Programs right at your ability level;

(2) Programs above your ability level, and (3) Programs that are below your ability level.

If you are only shooting for schools that will be a stretch, you are narrowing the possibility of being recruited and receiving a scholarship. Your ultimate objective is to go somewhere you will play and enjoy it, whether you receive a scholarship or not. And above all, receive a good education.

You should compile a list of 40-50 schools to contact. Your current "top list" may not be your top list when you get through the recruiting process. There are so many good schools and programs out there, most of which you are not familiar with right now. So keep your options open by contacting schools in all three of the above categories.

Q: What does it take to qualify to play for a college team? I know I have the ability.

A: The two things you need to focus on are academics and athletics. Both go hand in hand. You may have the ability to play at a major school, but if your grades do not qualify, you won't be recruited there.

You should definitely download the **Guide for the College Bound Student-Athlete** from both the NCAA and NAIA to help you understand the most important rules. This would be relevant in your case.

Q: Should we continue to send updated information to the entire list of schools that we sent to or only to those that have responded to us? And how often do we send updates? Can you give me examples of updates to send to the coaches?

A: Send updates to all the schools you have initially written to, assuming you have interest in each of those schools.

If you send an update to schools you have not yet heard from, attach the Profile again so they have the basic information. Send an update after each season, whether it be high school or club. Attach it to your email. The body of the email should be a short note to stand out and add that personal touch. It shows you are truly interested. Open it with something like, "You have my information on file, and I want to give you my latest update." There is a sample update in this book.

Q: I don't know if I could get a scholarship. My team was 0-10 last season.

A: Just because your team had a bad season, don't be discouraged from pursuing a scholarship. What matters most is your own play and stats. While it's always nice to be on a winning team, if you're a stand-out player with good stats in a league of strong competitors, you can get a scholarship even
if your team had a bad season. If you and your high school coach believe you can play well at the college level, you should go for it.

Q: I am graduating this month, but I still want to try for a football scholarship. What should I do, even though I am so late?

A: Here's my advice. You might go to a junior college while you begin the recruiting process for admission to a 4-year school for a year or two later. You can get good exposure and build your player skills and stats there, which will assist you in your football scholarship process. You'll also have another coach at an even higher level who can give you a reference and recommendation.

Q: My son's coach wants to write him a letter of recommendation. How important is that in the recruiting process?

A: That's good! It's a plus. Strategically, it will be best to send it when you send your introductory packet, so that you have everything together in one mailing/emailing. Otherwise, the coaches may not match up the two. They get a lot of mail and email.

Q: I am not being recruited because of my low ACT scores. What should I do?

A: As you have discovered, your academics are a big part in your ability to land a scholarship. If you are not being recruited because of your ACT scores, we would recommend spending a year or two at a Junior College to raise your grades and then pursuing a scholarship once you have the grades.

Q: When should I start the recruiting and scholarship process?

A: It is good to begin making contact with schools after your freshman year. You may not hear much from coaches until you are a junior, though, because that's the class they really focus on. However, if you've already established a relationship through your emails, profile, questionnaire and updates, you will stand out in the coach's mind. It is important that you send stats once you have varsity or club numbers.

Q: My son is good in more than one sport. Should he pursue a scholarship in each one, or focus on one sport?

A: If your son plays multiple sports and is talented in each, it would be wise to pursue recruiting in each of them. That is, in the ones he really wants to compete in at the college level. It keeps your options open. And, at some schools, he may have the chance to play two sports.

Q: How do I choose the right summer basketball camp where I can be recruited?

A: In choosing a basketball camp, it is best to find one where the schools you are interested in will be represented. Or ones where there will be many coaches there, so you will have a lot of exposure. The camps are expensive, so you need to choose wisely. Most schools use these as fundraisers for the program, so be selective. Ideally, you should go to a camp at a school which is near the top of your list.

Q: I don't live in the United States. Can I still get an athletic scholarship at a U.S. college?

A: International student-athletes have the same sports

scholarship opportunities at U.S. colleges. However, because of distance, unless they take the initiative they have a very difficult time getting noticed by the college recruiters. This book helps you deal with this distance drawback by teaching you how to proactively market yourself to the colleges you're interested in.

There are special eligibility standards that International students must be aware of, documented in NCAA's **Guide to International Academic Standards for Athletics Eligibility** (available online at NCAA's website).

Appendix D:
NCAA Recruiting and Eligibility Rules

Rules, rules, rules. The NCAA is the king of rules. But if you want to be recruited, you have to follow them. And so do the coaches who recruit you. We hear stories every year about schools who have been penalized for recruiting rules violations. This has cost schools millions of dollars in some cases, restrictions from post-season competition, loss of scholarships, and other serious sanctions.

So, it is good to be familiar with the rules so you understand "the game" before you start. The following information pertains to Division I rules. Division II and Division III is slightly different. Refer to the NCAA recruiting calendar for details. The web address is below.

General Recruiting Information

It all begins when you start ninth grade. That's when you become a prospective student-athlete. And you become a *recruited* student-athlete at a college if a coach or representative of the athletic program (including a booster) contacts you or a family member about you attending that school and participating in athletics. For a complete look at the NCAA recruiting calendars for all divisions, go to:

http://www.ncaa.org/student-athletes/resources/recruiting-calendars

What exactly does "contact" mean? It can include: (1) providing you with an "official visit", (2) placing more than one telephone call to you or a family member, or (3) visiting you or a family member anywhere other than on the college campus.

As stated officially on the NCAA website, "In addition to recruiting regulations, contacts may not be made by the school's alumni, boosters or representatives of their athletic program." That means no letters, phone calls or visits from boosters.

In addition, no cars or cash allowed! You or your family may not receive any inducements to encourage you to attend a certain school. These inducements include cash, clothing, cars, improper expenses, transportation, gifts or loans.

Evaluations

An "evaluation" is defined by the NCAA as "any off-campus activity used to assess your academic qualifications or your athletic ability, including a visit to your high school (during which no contact occurs) or watching you practice or compete at any site."

Official Visits

One of the most exciting things you can experience in your recruiting life is an "official visit." This is when a coach invites you to come to visit their campus and pays your way. You can have one expense-paid (official) visit to a particular college campus. And you can have a total of five official visits altogether. Your first official visit can occur beginning opening day of your senior year of classes.

If you are being recruited for more than one sport, this five-visit limit applies. Therefore, whether you are a one-sport athlete or multi-sport, do not use up your five visits too early. As you can see, there is strategy to all this.

There is a pre-requisite for making an official visit. You must have a Certification Account with the NCAA Eligibility Center before you can go on an official visit.

Your official visit may not exceed 48 hours. This expense-paid trip can include round-trip transportation for you and your parents or legal guardians, plus meals, lodging and complimentary admission to campus athletic events.

The NCAA also has restrictions on what printed material the school can provide you with through the mail or on your official visit. You'll gain a collection of college catalogs, game programs, media guides, schedules and student-athlete handbooks.

As you can see, coaches have a lot of rules to follow. The above information is provided as a summary and the NCAA can change these rules at any time. We recommend you go to the NCAA website and view the rules in the **Guide for the College Bound Student-Athlete**.

Contact, Evaluation, Quiet and Dead Periods

Keeping all the dates in mind, there's another twist to the whole calendar. There are four periods coaches much adhere to in recruiting. Keep these in mind, because it will explain why you are hearing from coaches in some times and why you aren't in others. Click on your sport on the page below in order to see when the periods are in your sport:

http://www.ncaa.org/student-athletes/resources/recruiting-calendars

The NCAA does a good job defining the periods:

Contact period: During a contact period, a college coach may have face-to-face contact with college-bound student-athletes or their parents, watch student-athletes compete and visit their high schools, and write or telephone student-athletes or their parents.

Evaluation period: During an evaluation period, a college coach may watch college-bound student-athletes compete, visit their high schools, and write or telephone student-athletes or their parents. However, a college coach may not have face-to-face contact with college-bound student-athletes or their parents off the college's campus during an evaluation period.

Quiet period: During a quiet period, a college coach may only have face-to-face contact with college-bound student-athletes or their parents on the college's campus. A coach may not watch student-athletes compete (unless a competition occurs on the college's campus) or visit their high schools. Coaches may write or telephone college-bound student-athletes or their parents during this time.

146

Dead period: During a dead period, a college coach may not have face-to-face contact with college-bound student-athletes or their parents, and may not watch student-athletes compete or visit their high schools. Coaches may write and telephone student-athletes or their parents during a dead period.

Eligibility

You have to meet certain academic requirements before you can be eligible to compete in intercollegiate athletics. This eligibility pertains to all athletes, regardless of whether you are seeking a scholarship or not. In other words, you have to meet the requirements before you can step on the field at all.

The NCAA has set up an **Eligibility Center**, which has been discussed in detail earlier in this book. http://eligibilitycenter.org.

Changes in SAT/ACT Tests

SAT and ACT both made changes in their tests, adding a third "writing" (essay) section. It's a mandatory section for the SAT, but is optional for the ACT.

So how did this test change impact NCAA eligibility requirements? Not at all (yet). NCAA decided not to pay attention to the writing component scores - for the present time. They will just use the combined scores from the "reading" and "math" sections for the SAT score requirements, ignoring the "writing" section score. This means there is still a maximum of 1600 on the SAT scores - just as before this change. For the ACT, the "writing" section is optional, so the ACT combined scores have remained the same.

Division I Initial Eligibility

To be a qualifying student-athlete and be eligible to compete in intercollegiate athletics at the Division I level:

1. You must graduate from high school.

2. Successfully complete a core curriculum of at least 16 academic course units as follows:

   - English: 4 years
   - Natural or physical science (including at least one lab course if offered by the high school): 2 years
   - Mathematics (Algebra I or higher): 3 years
   - Additional courses in English, math, or natural or physical science: 1 year
   - Social science: 2 years
   - Additional academic courses (in any of the above areas or foreign language, philosophy or non-doctrinal religion --such as comparative religion): 4 years

3. Meet the standards of the following formula: have a core-course GPA (based on a 4.0 max) and a combined score on the SAT reading and math sections or a sum score on the ACT based on the "qualifier index scale." This scale is charted below. What's it going to show you? Basically that if your core GPA is poor, your SAT and ACT scores must be higher for you to qualify.

The test score/GPA requirements for D1 and D2 levels are charted in detail on the NCAA website:

http://www.ncaa.org/student-athletes/future/test-scores

Division II Initial Eligibility

The eligibility requirements for a Division II school are as follows:

1. Graduate from high school.

2. Have a **GPA of 2.0 or higher** (2.2 beginning 8/1/18) in a successfully completed core curriculum of at least 16 academic course units:

   - English: 3 years
   - Math: 2 years (Algebra I or higher)
   - Natural or physical science (including 1 year of lab): 2 years
   - Additional courses in English, math or natural or physical science: 3 years
   - Social science: 2 years
   - Additional academic courses (in any of the above areas or foreign language, or philosophy or non-doctrinal religion): 4 years

3. Have a minimum **SAT score of 820** or a **sum ACT score of 68**.

NOTE: Beginning 8/1/18, you need to earn an SAT combined score or ACT sum score matching your core-course GPA on the Division II sliding scale. See the chart at http://www.ncaa.org/student-athletes/future/test-scores.

There is "partial qualifier" status in Division II. You are eligible to practice, but not compete against other schools. You then have four seasons of eligibility remaining. You are also eligible to receive an athletic scholarship during the first year.

The requirements for a partial qualifier at a Division II school are as follows: You must graduate from high school and meet one of these requirements: (1) Minimum SAT or ACT scores indicated above, or (2) successful completion of the required core curriculum above, consisting of 16 core courses with a 2.00 GPA in the core.

Division III Initial Eligibility

There are no athletic scholarships at the Division III level. This is no reflection on the quality of those schools. Many Division III schools are ranked among the top schools in the nation.

Eligibility for financial aid, practice and competition is governed by the school, conference, or other NCAA rules. You should contact the schools for more information.

A final note on Initial Eligibility

The standards I've discussed here are merely the minimum NCAA standards for athletic eligibility. The school may have tougher requirements, and your entrance requirements and admission are determined by them. Finally, the GED test may be used under certain conditions to satisfy the graduation requirement, but, of course, you will still need to meet the SAT and ACT test score standards.

The information in this Appendix is for general information purposes. Full details on rules and regulations can be found in the *Guide for the College-Bound Student Athlete*. You can go online to the

NCAA website to view and download the latest versions.

Foreign Student Eligibility

Foreign (international) student-athletes are also eligible for athletic scholarships at U.S. colleges, but the eligibility standards vary depending on the country. NCAA has a document that gives most of the details a foreign student-athlete will need, country by country: **Guide to International Academic Standards for Athletics Eligibility**. This is available online, along with other resources, at the NCAA website:

http://www.ncaapublications.com/productdownloads/IS1516.pdf

This is the latest edition at the time of this book going to press (2017). If this is not the latest copy, replace "1516" in the url with the current school year.

If you've never been enrolled as a full-time student in a university: You must meet minimum academic standards in order to be eligible (the ones that vary by country). You will also need a minimum score on the SAT or the ACT. Other tests, such as the TOEFL or the TWSE, are not accepted.

If you have been or are currently enrolled as a full-time student at a university in a foreign country: You will be considered a transfer student, and your eligibility will follow the normal NCAA Transfer Guide rules. This is available online, at the NCAA website:

https://www.ncaapublications.com/searchadv.aspx?IsSubmit=true&SearchTerm=transfer%20guide

As I said earlier, NCAA has a lot of rules, and they publish almost all their rules online. Unfortunately, many student-athletes have difficulty finding the information they're seeking just because there's so much on the NCAA website.

With that warning in advance, we want to advise you that there's a wealth of information available online from the NCAA. If you need to know specifics or answers to more unusual questions, you can probably find the answer on the NCAA website.

You can contact the NCAA at:

National Collegiate Athletic Association
700 W. Washington St.
PO Box 6222
Indianapolis, IN 46206-6222
(317) 917-6222

www.ncaa.org

You can contact the NCAA Initial Eligibility
Clearinghouse at:

www.eligibilitycenter.org
or toll-free at 877-262-1492

NAIA Recruiting and Eligibility Rules

NAIA rules and regulations are a lot less complicated. Let's get right into them.

Scholarships

Like the NCAA, the NAIA controls the number of scholarships available per sport. You can combine academic and athletic scholarships in the NAIA, as in the NCAA, but academic scholarships could count against the team's athletic scholarship limit.

Basically, there is more money available in the NAIA. However, most NAIA schools are private schools, and the cost to attend is much higher on the average. Therefore, the final cost to you could be comparable or even higher than an NCAA state school.

With our sons, they both had academic and athletic scholarship offers at NAIA schools, and the net cost to us would have been $15,000-$25,000 per year.

Scholarships are administered according to the policies of the school, not the NAIA, as long as they stay within the limits per sport.

Recruiting

One huge difference between the NCAA and NAIA recruiting rules is that in the NAIA **you are able to**

have a workout with the team. This is a tremendous opportunity, and we recommend you take advantage of that. You get to see the coach, meet the team, see how you like the program in action, and it allows the coach to assess your abilities. Your tryout must be done on campus. The NAIA even allows you to have an individual tryout apart from the team practice, but we recommend the former.

Eligibility

In order to be eligible to participate in a scrimmage or intercollegiate competition, you have to fulfill the following:

Meet two of the following three requirements upon entering as a Freshman:

1. Score a minimum of 18 on the ACT or 860 SAT (Critical Reading and Math), if taken before March 2016;
   940 SAT (Evidence-Based Reading and Writing + Math), if taken in March 2016 or after.
2. Have a high school GPA of 2.0 on a 4.0 scale.
3. Graduate in the top half of your high school class.

Once entering an NAIA school, you have to keep up with the work and perform well. Detailed requirements can be found on the NAIA website.

The NAIA makes this statement regarding recruiting, setting it apart from the NCAA:

"The NAIA recruiting process for both freshmen and transfers is less cumbersome, with few restrictions on the contact between a student-athlete and a coach. More

frequent communication allows the student to become more comfortable with the school and athletics staff."

[A Guide for the College-Bound Athlete]

The NAIA rules hold strict academic requirements. Recruits must register with the Eligibility Center, which was established in 2010.

The NAIA can be reached at:
National Association of Intercollegiate Athletics
1200 Grand Blvd.
Kansas City, MO 64106
(816) 595-8000

ww.naia.org

NAIA Eligibility Center

https://www.playnaia.org/eligibility-center

About Recruit-Me

Recruit-Me is a premier entity helping student-athlete families pursue an athletic scholarship. While many companies have come and gone over the years, Recruit-Me has stood the test of time, since 2002, because families are getting results.

Recruit-Me has this distinctive:

We empower families to carry out the recruiting process on their own. This not only saves families money, but gives them full control of this extremely important endeavor.

Secondly, we teach a systematic, step-by-step approach. This not only saves families time, but keeps them from getting confused, discouraged or lost.

In addition, our resources have always been affordable. From free to a couple hundred dollars.

At the heart of what we do is the personal commitment to help families succeed. The founder and CEO, Jon Fugler, is a parent who went through the process personally and then with his kids. This is a family business.

Learn more about Recruit-Me at **www.recruit-me.com**.

About the Author

Jon Fugler, CEO of **Recruit-Me,** has been coaching families through the athletic scholarship process since 2002. It all started when his twin sons were seeking athletic scholarships a few years earlier.

With a daughter already in college, he and his wife knew that they needed financial help. Their sons were talented athletes, so the family received counsel and coaching from a seasoned expert. Both boys landed a fully paid education at the school of their choice.

Soon after, Jon co-founded Recruit-Me, and since then he has helped thousands of families navigate the recruiting process. Jon has spoken to parent and athlete groups, has conducted many multi-media recruiting classes and seminars, has developed the acclaimed **Recruit-Me Athletic Scholarship System**, and is the founder of **Athletic Scholarship University**, the only step-by-step course available for student-athletes and parents.

He is also host of the weekly **Athletic Scholarship Podcast.**

Jon and his wife, Noonie, live in Colorado. They have three children and seven grandchildren.

You can contact Jon at **jon@recruit-me.com** or tweet him @jonfugler.

Invite Jon to Speak

Jon enjoys speaking to groups of parents and athletes to help them succeed in their scholarship efforts. If you'd like to schedule him to come in person or to present via Skype, he is available for limited engagements. You can contact Jon at **jon@recruit-me.com** or call (719) 270-1346.

Pursuing Next Steps

Advice from Jon

Now that you've read the Playbook, you have the resources to pursue your athletic scholarship dream. If you've taken action on a couple of the steps I've shared with you, then you're already on your way.

Please, please, stick with it and you'll be rewarded.

It's true that thousands of families in this month alone will start the journey to get an athletic scholarship.

However, only a few (a very few) will succeed wildly.

A few more will get stuck in the sad mud of mediocrity, neither experiencing the thrill of victory nor the agony of defeat. These will live in "no man's land".

Most will fail. Miserably and repeatedly. When I say "most", I mean at least 97%.

But they don't have the Playbook that you have in your hands.

What most families do is spend tons of money on travel, camps, club teams and tournaments—I mean thousands of dollars—hoping their kid will be seen and recruited.

Or they hire out the recruiting process to a third party or a faceless service.

Or, worst of all, they get advice from other parents who haven't even succeeded at getting their kids scholarships.

For most families, none of that works. They get discouraged along the way and give up out of frustration or confusion.

Their son or daughter gets to the end of their senior year with no offers ... their talented athlete doesn't get to compete past high school on scholarship ... the family has just one or two inferior choices ... and the parents are stuck with a huge college bill ahead of them. I've seen it over and over again.

Maybe you know what it's like to set out for your goal with enthusiasm, only to strike out time and time again.

You do your very best to get your athlete on coaches' radars, but they end up getting zero attention instead. Or that initial interest turned out to be a form letter or email blast to hundreds of kids.

Does any of this sound familiar?

Don't feel bad - you're not alone, and it's not your fault.

The very fact that you've read this Playbook puts you in a different category. You have the knowledge. You just need to put it into action.

Yet, you may still feel you're lacking something. Knowledge doesn't equal success.

I've worked with many families over the years that have asked me to personally walk them **step-by-step** through the recruiting process ... all the way to an athletic scholarship.

That's why I created **Athletic Scholarship University**. This six-module multi-media course has a wealth of resources, including on-demand video with me as your instructor.

Athletic Scholarship University is based on the Recruit-Me Athletic Scholarship System, the step-by-step system used by my families for over 15 years.

Every module has bonus resources that support each of the steps I'll go through with you in the video sessions.

Find out more at:

www.AthleticScholarshipUniversity.com

With this resource, I will lead you through the recruiting steps. You might need this extra push. That way, you won't just put this book down or get distracted or discouraged along the way.

The truth is, every great accomplishment involves going beyond what the rest of the world is doing and going after it *differently* than the average person.

There's no reason holding you back from the same kind of success that scholarship families enjoy.

If you feel you need help implementing this Playbook, I've created Athletic Scholarship University for that purpose.

I take any confusion out of your recruiting process. When families gain clarity, it lifts their results to a whole new level. Coaches pursue the student-athlete and there is no longer any problem getting on a lot of coaches' radars ... and staying there!

I have seen it work for over 15 years. My greatest reward is the success of my families. Here's what they have said about Recruit-Me:

"I strongly feel your program helped my son receive a full scholarship to college. The way you structured the information made it a lot easier for us to "screen" potential schools down to the ones that best matched the school's needs to my son's needs."
Joe C., California

"I have loved the whole program because it gave me an opportunity to maintain a level of control over my son's future. This program is great and I would like to encourage more parents to become more involved in allowing their child to realize his/her dream."
Robert, Alabama

"In my daughter's case, Recruit-Me helped her to successfully showcase her athletic skills that resulted in her now competing at an elite New England college. In her words, 'I am living my dream.' Thank you for the help and on-going support." *David, Utah*

After you have spent just a short time working through the recruiting steps in Athletic Scholarship University, what once appeared dark and mysterious will suddenly become clear, simple and intuitive!

This Playbook in your hands was designed for families to take control of the recruiting process on their own. If that's you, move ahead.

If you need more help from me, then check out Athletic Scholarship University at:

www.AthleticScholarshipUniversity.com

In any case, I want to hear how things go for you. Please send me an email with your story to **jon@recruit-me.com.**

Made in the USA
Middletown, DE
08 August 2018